PRAISE FOR
The Heart Path of Mary Magdalene

"Reading *The Heart Path of Mary Magdalene*, I felt I had been transported into a world of mystic women's insight. The wisdom streaming from this book is both earthy-useful and universally expanding my mind."

—**Kelly Bryson**, author of *Don't Be Nice, Be Real*

"An excellent guide to applying and living Mary Magdalene's heart-centered teachings—from a woman who deeply understands these teachings."

—**Suvani Stepanek**, coauthor of *Grow Your Healthy Relationship Cards*

"This is my favorite book from Mercedes so far! Mercedes shares her secret ingredients to the recipe of 'How to Connect to Your Divinity.' Read this book and enjoy the beautiful blessings of the Magdalene."

—**Rachel Goodwin**, author of *Sarah's Little Book of Healing*

"Award-winning author and channel Mercedes Kirkel once again brings Mary Magdalene to vibrant life in *The Heart Path of Mary Magdalene*. Reading these teachings is like sitting with a trusted counselor who knows your heart and illuminates your personal path through the mundane to the spiritual."

—**Carly Newfeld**, producer and host, *"The Last Word: Conversations with Writers"*

"*The Heart Path of Mary Magdalene* deepens our connection with Mary Magdalene's messages of love, offering practical steps for living Mary's guidance. Kirkel invites us to a clearer, truer, more loving version of ourselves."

—**Loren Swift**, author of *The Earth Keeper's Handbook*

"This book is a fantastic resource for anyone who would like to go deeper into their relationships and themselves. It has the potential to revolutionize how people speak and, more importantly, how they listen, enabling richer and more meaningful lives."

—Kevin Miller, author and filmmaker

"If you want to inhabit wisdom, this book is a must!"

—Rosemary Eads, psychotherapist

"Mercedes Kirkel has woven the divine wisdom of Mary Magdalene with the grounding of exercises. This practical workbook inspires and guides."

—Francesca Gentille, coauthor of *The Marriage of Sex & Spirit*

The Heart Path of
MARY MAGDALENE

A Guide to
Living from Your Heart

Mercedes Kirkel

INTO THE HEART
Creations

RIO RANCHO, NEW MEXICO

Published by
INTO THE HEART CREATIONS
Rio Rancho, New Mexico
www.intotheheart.org

Copyright © 2022 by Mercedes Kirkel

All rights reserved. No part of this book may be used or reproduced in any manner whatsoever without written permission, except in the case of brief quotations embedded in critical articles and reviews.

First edition

Printed in the United States of America

Names:	Kirkel, Mercedes, author.
Title:	The Heart Path of Mary Magdalene : a guide to living from your heart / Mercedes Kirkel.
Description:	First edition.	Rio Rancho, New Mexico : Into the Heart Creations, [2022]	Series: The Magdalene-Yeshua teachings ; book 4.
Identifiers:	ISBN: 978-0-9840029-8-6 (paperbook)	978-0-9840029-9-3 (ebook)	LCCN: 2022901873
Subjects:	LCSH: Mary Magdalene, Saint (Spirit)	Self-actualization (Psychology)	Inspiration.	Spiritual life.	Spirituality.	Mind and body.	Peace of mind.	Mindfulness (Psychology)	Emotions.	Emotional conditioning.	Spirit writings.	Channeling (Spiritualism)	Jesus Christ--Spiritualistic interpretations.	Jesus Christ--New Age movement interpretations.	Jesus Christ--Family.	BISAC: BODY, MIND & SPIRIT / Inspiration & Personal Growth.	BODY, MIND & SPIRIT / Channeling & Mediumship.	BODY, MIND & SPIRIT / Angels & Spirit Guides.	BODY, MIND & SPIRIT / Mindfulness & Meditation.	BODY, MIND & SPIRIT / Goddess Worship.	BODY, MIND & SPIRIT / Ancient Mysteries & Controversial Knowledge.
Classification:	LCC: BS2485 .K572 2022	DDC: 226/.092--dc23

Book design by Michelle M. White

Your open heart is the most powerful vessel of transformation,
of receiving divine light and empowering it with love.

—Mary Magdalene

Mary Magdalene Beckons: Join the River of Love

Contents

Introduction 3

1. *Remove Judgment and Blame* 9
   - The Downside of Blame and Judgment 10
   - We Were Trained to Judge 13
   - Recognizing Judgment and Blame 14
   - Judgment Words 18
   - Pure Observation 19
   - Expressing the Stimulus 21
   - The Self-Judgment Stage 23
   - What Nonjudgment Isn't 24
   - Practice 27

2. *Grow Your Feeling Ability* 29
   - Common Beliefs about Feelings 31
   - The Gift of Pain 34
   - Building Your "Feeling Muscle" 35
   - Joyful Feelings 37
   - Painful Feelings 38
   - Opening to Feelings 40
   - Two Ways 43
   - Non-Feelings 46
   - Hybrid Feelings 48
   - Freeing the Heart 49
   - Practice 50

3. *Connect to Your Inner Divinity* 51
   Understanding Inner Divinity 52
   Inner Divine Qualities 53
   Outer Events Don't Cause Our Feelings 55
   Which Inner Divine Quality Needs Attention? 57
   Inner Divine Qualities Are Universal 60
   Crossing the Bridge to God 61
   Match the Feeling and the Inner Divine Quality 63
   The Shift into Peace 65
   Next Steps 66
   Practice 67

4. *Ask for What You Want* 69
   Respect Free Will 71
   Helping Others 74
   Skills for Making Requests 76
   Free Will with Children 79
   Practice 82

5. *Respond from Your Heart* 83
   Typical Responses 84
   A Different Way to Respond 87
   Heart-Listening 87
   Heart-Reflecting 89
   Skills for Heart-Responding 91
   Less Is More 93
   Matching Intensity 94
   Toned-Down Feelings 95
   When Both People Are in Pain 97
   Heart-Responding to Children 98
   Practice 99

6. *Include Everyone* 101
    Abundance Consciousness 103
    Dominators and Submitters 104
    More Skills for Inclusion 108
    Receive Abundantly 110
    Apologize from Your Heart 112
    Celebrations and Mournings 113
    Practice 114

Resources 117
    12 Steps of the Heart Path—Principles 118
    12 Steps of the Heart Path—Practices 119
    Heart-Expressing 120
    Heart-Reflecting 121
    Judgment Words 122
    Joyful Feelings 123
    Painful Feelings 124
    Toned-Down Feelings 126
    Inner Divine Qualities 129

Notes 131

About the Author 133

Books and Videos by Mercedes Kirkel 135

The Heart Path of
MARY MAGDALENE

Introduction

I am a channel for Mary Magdalene[1] and Yeshua.[2] For those not familiar with channeling, a channel is someone who communicates with beings in other realms or dimensions. I'm also the author of *Mary Magdalene Beckons: Join the River of Love* (book one of the Yeshua-Magdalene Teachings),[3] which this book is based on.

When *Mary Magdalene Beckons* was released, many people were deeply moved by the communication and teaching from Mary that they found in that book. However, during my private sessions with individuals, it became clear that most people didn't understand how to apply Mary's wisdom in their lives. That's what inspired me to create the Heart Path of Mary Magdalene course—to help people use Mary's wisdom to change their lives. This book evolved out of that course and my one-on-one sessions.

I want to explain that I used to teach Nonviolent Communication (NVC).[4] If you're familiar with NVC, you'll notice that I've integrated many NVC ideas and practices into this book. In fact, early in the process of receiving Mary's messages, I became aware that Mary seemed to be including NVC principles in her communications. At first that surprised and concerned me. *Perhaps this wasn't Mary Magdalene speaking at all. Maybe it was just me bringing forth my own ideas!*

Over time as I became more familiar with the way channeling works, I realized that Mary was making use of concepts in my own mind to bring forth the ideas that *she* wanted to elucidate. I believe this is the way all higher beings work when they communicate through someone else. The channel—in this case, me—makes their mind available for the higher being. The higher being then uses the channel's language, ideas, and thought patterns to give form to what the higher being wants to convey. Because of this I came to see that it was natural, perhaps even inevitable, that some of my ideas would appear in Mary's communications.

On a deeper level, I was coming to view my whole life as preparation for my role as a channel for Mary Magdalene. In this light, my training in NVC was an integral part of that preparation. I saw that NVC principles and practices work exceedingly well as tools to understand and apply Mary's teaching. I've learned over the years of channeling Mary that she's eminently practical. I think she chose to build on NVC concepts and methods because they're deeply effective in connecting people with their heart. In my own life, and in the lives of countless clients, I've seen this to be the case.

I do experience one important difference between the two teachings, however. NVC is often used to improve relationships and resolve conflicts, while Mary's messages and instructions are, first and foremost, about helping us to grow and deepen in God. She uses NVC teachings as a means to help us connect more deeply with the divine.[5]

I'm now at a place of trust and deep appreciation regarding the blending of NVC with Mary's work. I believe my NVC background combines with Mary's path in a wonderful marriage. NVC provides Mary's exalted teaching with a set of hands-on tools that are practical and grounded. This "marriage" supports the intention that Mary Magdalene and Marshall Rosenberg share: to help us live from the heart.

Why is living from the heart important? The heart holds many treasures. It's the source of love. It leads us to peace. It's an access-way to inner guidance. Perhaps most importantly, shifting from the head to the heart (as our base and the place where we're centered) is a major component of our spiritual evolution. This shift from head to heart sets the stage for our transition into higher dimensions of being.

Mary's use of the word "dimension" is different from the scientific reference to the first, second, third, or fourth dimensions. Mary uses the term to mean a particular realm or plane of reality. According to Mary, our universe has twelve dimensions, with most of humanity currently residing in the third dimension. Mary is dedicated to helping us move into the fourth dimension and beyond. She calls this the *ascension process*.[6]

You can look at the ascension process as a spiritual school for evolving consciousness. When we've completed our soul work in a certain dimension, which includes mastering the consciousness associated with that level, we move on to the next higher dimension. In third-dimensional reality (3D), our primary learning relates to power, and our consciousness is based on *power-over*. At this level the mind is the principal means and instrument for acquiring and maintaining power over others. When we move into the fourth dimension (4D), our consciousness changes into *power-with*. At this level we're guided by the heart rather than the mind, and we naturally relate to others inclusively. We include rather than exclude others.

While consciousness can be a vague or confusing concept for many, Mary's approach is, once again, very practical. What we say is used as an avenue to access our consciousness. (This includes the things we say silently in our head.) Think of it this way: our speech is a window into our consciousness. Or, to put it another way, if we want to understand our consciousness, we can look at our speech. Mary takes this idea a step further, using our speech as a tool for changing our consciousness. Our verbal expression becomes a form of spiritual practice and transformation, supporting us in becoming the people we want to be.

This is deep work. In learning this material, I urge you to be gentle with yourself. It can be disheartening to observe your consciousness through the window of your words, only to discover that you're not as spiritually advanced as you thought you were. However, awareness is the first step toward change. If you continue with the practices presented in these pages, I'm confident you'll see yourself grow in ways you desire. I've witnessed it again and again in myself and in the many people I've supported in learning and integrating Mary's teaching.

One of the things that can support you in maintaining a disposition of gentleness and self-compassion is to remember that Mary is presenting a spiritual practice. Just as you wouldn't expect to master Buddhism after taking your first course in Buddhist principles, so it is with this work. Each reading of this material will deepen your understanding of Mary's path and affect you in new ways. Each encounter with this work will provide something that you specifically need. But the greatest transformation and benefit will come through engaging this path in your life.

Rather than reading this book straight through from start to finish, I urge you to spend a week on each chapter. Let each portion of the material settle in before going on. Think of yourself as being on a six-week spiritual retreat, with each week having a different focus. Notice how the material for each week relates to your daily life and how it's changing you. After completing your six-week retreat, I suggest that you return to this book periodically as an ongoing resource and guide for walking Mary's heart path.

For even deeper integration, I recommend taking the Heart Path video course,[7] in which I demonstrate the principles presented in this book with a group of people. Each video corresponds to one chapter in this book. Through practice exercises and real-life situations, the video course shows what the heart path looks like in real life. You can include the videos as part of your six-week retreat, or you can take the video course after completing this book.

I also recommend reading the source text for this material, *Mary Magdalene Beckons: Join the River of Love*.[8] If you've already read *Mary Magdalene Beckons*, I urge you to revisit it after studying this material. I'm confident you'll get even more out of it.

Finally, this book can be used as a study guide for a practice group. Invite participants to share their understanding of the material and their life experiences that relate to that topic.

In writing down everything contained here, my hope is that I'm replacing myself. To the best of my ability, I've included all the skills and techniques that I use when I coach people in how to live Mary's heart path. Now I pass the torch to you. May you be well supported through all that's within these pages to live from your heart.

ONE

Remove Judgment and Blame

> **MARY MAGDALENE:** Meditating on the wrongness of others is ... keeping you a prisoner of your own mind, locked away from your heart. And your heart holds the key to all else, to all the doors to your higher awakening.
>
> *Mary Magdalene Beckons*, "Opening the Heart," pp. 199-200

Mary Magdalene's heart path is a spiritual practice. It helps us live from the heart and supports our higher spiritual awakening. Like most spiritual paths, it involves certain disciplines or practices. These disciplines come in two forms: 1) things we agree not to do and 2) things we commit to doing. These disciplines fuel our spiritual growth and transformation.

In the heart path, the initial practice is to stop blaming and judging. Many of us regularly engage in judgment and blame, often without realizing it. Releasing these habits allows for a different kind of engagement—a heart-based relating to ourselves, others, and God.

Because the patterns of blame and judgment are often deeply ingrained, this first step can feel like unlearning. We're becoming aware of something we've done unconsciously for most of our lives. Now we're consciously choosing to abstain from those habitual behaviors.

The word "judgment" here is meant in a particular way. Judgment indicates that something is right or wrong, good or bad. When we judge, we're adding an interpretation to an event. Blame adds an additional component that often accompanies judgment. Blame is pointing to someone or something as the cause of the rightness or wrongness—it's their fault.

The Downside of Blame and Judgment

MARY MAGDALENE: The whole game of right and wrong is a huge obstacle to receiving love or to being love. If you have learned that game, as so many of you have, you must now undo that thinking within yourself.

Mary Magdalene Beckons, "From Blame to Love," pp. 242-243

Judgment and blame bring a number of problems. The most readily noticeable one is that they result in living in our mind, with much of our mental activity going into determining who's right and who's wrong. What's more, we believe that our opinions as to what's right and wrong are right!

I used to have the sense that my ideas of right and wrong were backed up by an authority that I was sure existed. I visualized this validating authority as a panel of judges, situated slightly above my head, nodding in agreement with my judgments. It was as though they were implicitly telling me: *You have the inside track as to what's right and what's wrong. You are uniquely correct in your assessment of rightness and wrongness in a way that no one else is.*

I think many of us can relate to this idea that we're the one who *really* knows, and our viewpoint is "right." If others disagree, they're "wrong." This is where a great deal of conflict and suffering comes from. When we think we're right and others are wrong, we put ourselves in the position of "me versus you."

Other problems also come from the habit of judging. When we judge we focus on "the other" rather than ourselves. All of our attention and energy is directed outward, toward others. This external focus makes us dependent on outside forces for our happiness. If others caused "it" (whatever "it" may be in a given situation), we depend on them to change it. But we don't usually have power over others or external forces. By focusing on others, we give our power away and become victims.

Furthermore, our external focus diverts us from what's going on with us. Throughout *Mary Magdalene Beckons,* Mary emphasizes how essential it is to be connected to our feelings and inner life. This is where our true power and purpose reside. Living in our mind and focusing on externals takes us away from our spiritual work and from receiving the gifts of that work.

Judging creates a world of stratification. Whoever (or whatever) is seen as right or good is upheld as superior and deserving; whoever (or whatever) is wrong or bad is derogated as inferior and undeserving. All of this reinforces separation in consciousness and experience.

Needing to be right creates stress. If being right means receiving the rewards of winning, and perhaps even of being loved, then it is vital to be right; you may even feel as though your very survival depends on it. By replacing judgment and blame with heart-based practices, we release a great deal of stress, freeing up energy for well-being and spiritual growth.

There's one more consequence of living in your mind and judging things as right or wrong, one that from Mary's point of view is the most important: it keeps us from connecting to God. When we replace blame and judgment with a different pathway—through our feelings and into our inner life—we tremendously support our connection to God.

> **MARY MAGDALENE:** You are inherently motivated toward union with God because your soul remembers that bliss, that ecstasy, and continually longs for it in the depth of your being. Judging others through blame and criticism takes you away from that bliss, that ecstasy.
>
> *Mary Magdalene Beckons*, "Choosing the True God," pp. 219-220

Mary Magdalene is profoundly committed to helping us shift out of judgment and living in our head. She makes it clear that judgment and blame are not necessary, and they don't serve us. Instead, Mary guides us into our heart, beyond the dualism of experiencing life in two camps as either good or bad, right or wrong.

We Were Trained to Judge

> **MARY MAGDALENE:** Wrong and right are simply fabrications of your mind, ideas that have been created to try to get people to do certain things that some people want them to do. Can you imagine living without the thoughts that some things are right or wrong? It is entirely possible and would benefit you tremendously.
>
> *Mary Magdalene Beckons,* "The Joy of Forgiveness," p. 207

For most of us, the ideas of right and wrong were instilled from a young age. Our parents or caregivers taught us right and wrong, rewarding us when we were "good" and punishing us when we were "bad." This programming is reinforced throughout our lives, most often through speech imbued with judgment and blame. Right versus wrong thinking is also maintained through social institutions, such as schools, religions, media, and the legal system. Cultures frequently have ideas of right and wrong woven into them. Certain things are deemed appropriate or inappropriate, proper or improper, worthy or unworthy, and so on.

Yet living in judgment and blame is not our natural state. If you listen to young children who haven't yet received this training, you'll notice that they don't include judgment. They simply describe what happened. ("He took my ball" vs. "He was being mean.") In this regard, children can be our teachers, modeling how to communicate (and thus think) without adding judgment or blame.

The concept that right and wrong doesn't exist as an external reality can be unsettling. It can challenge what you think is real, as well as how you relate to your experience. Even more disturbing is the realization that these habits are deeply embedded in your thinking. If you find this to be the case, I urge you to be gentle with yourself. You didn't learn to judge overnight, and most likely it will take time to unlearn these habits and replace them with something new. Remember that awareness of your current patterns is the first step toward change. Just don't stop there. The real shift occurs when you replace those patterns with something else. That's what we'll be focusing on in the rest of the book.

Recognizing Judgment and Blame

> **MARY MAGDALENE:** Let go of your thinking-barricade that others or yourself have done something wrong, and stand vulnerable in your heart. See what you experience. See if God exists and if God loves you.
>
> *Mary Magdalene Beckons,* "From Blame to Love," p. 243

Let's look at some practical examples of judgment and blame. As you read these examples, notice how you feel. Most of us experience a characteristic feeling when we hear a judgment, whether we're the one judging or the judgment is coming from another. Recognizing this feeling can help us become aware of judgments.

A judgment can be as simple as saying that something is right or wrong, good or bad:

"You're wrong."
"I'm right."
"That's good."
"That's bad."

These are black-and-white examples of adding a judgment or interpretation to a situation. But judgments are often more subtle.

One way that judgments show up is when we begin a sentence with "I feel . . ." and then follow that with a judgment. When we do this, we're not actually expressing a feeling. We're expressing a thought with an added implication of rightness or wrongness. Here are some examples:

"I feel misunderstood."
"I feel betrayed."
"I feel attacked."
"I feel abandoned."
"I feel dismissed."
"I feel abused."
"I feel disrespected."
"I feel ignored."
"I feel cheated."
"I feel lied to."
"I feel left out."
"I feel attacked."
"I feel blamed."
"I feel dumped on."
"I feel insulted."
"I feel intimidated."
"I feel put down."

What these statements have in common is that they're not about us. They describe an action by someone else. Each of these communications is really about *what someone else is doing to us*.

The second thing that makes these sentences judgments is that each one has a connotation added to it, indicating that the other person is doing something bad or wrong. We're subtly communicating that the other "shouldn't be doing that" or "should be doing something else." The concepts of "should" and "shouldn't" are another way of conveying rightness and wrongness; "should" shows the right thing to do and "shouldn't" the wrong thing to do.

We also express judgment when we say (or think) *what someone or something is*. "He or she is . . .":

rude
immature
selfish
dishonest
oversensitive
too generous
a procrastinator
ugly
beautiful

Even what we might call a "positive" characterization—compliments or praise—is still a judgment if we're interpreting that the other person is good or right. Whether someone is regarded as ugly or beautiful, we're still projecting our judgment onto something or someone else, and we're still implying that they're either good or bad, right or wrong.

Sometimes we judge ourselves:

"I'm stupid."
"I'm smart."
"I'm fat."
"I'm not good enough."
"I'm great."
"I'm a failure."

In these statements, we turn ourselves into an object or other. We then proclaim what we are or aren't, with an added implication of goodness or badness.

Judgments occur when we describe an action as good or bad, right or wrong. In these cases, our sentences usually begin with "*That is . . .*":

"That is inappropriate."
"That is irresponsible."
"That is wrong."
"That is impossible."
"That's a bad habit."

Once again, these statements carry an interpretation that something is bad or wrong. It would also be a judgment if it was saying that something is good or right:

"That's the greatest."

Another common form of judgment is to *exaggerate or make universal statements*:

"You always . . ."
"They never . . ."

Unless such universal statements ("always" or "never") are factually true, they're most often employed to build a case and thus prove rightness or wrongness.

Judgment Words

abandoned	insulted	rejected
abused	interrupted	ripped off
attacked	intimidated	shut down
belittled	invalidated	shut out
betrayed	invisible	taken advantage of
blamed	isolated	threatened
bullied	judged	thwarted
cheated	left out	trampled on
coerced	manipulated	tricked
cornered	mistrusted	unappreciated
criticized	misunderstood	unheard
disliked	neglected	unloved
dismissed	overpowered	unseen
distrusted	overworked	unsupported
dumped on	patronized	unwanted
harassed	pressured	used
hassled	provoked	victimized
ignored	put down	violated

appropriate/ inappropriate	good/poor taste	superb/terrible
excellent/poor	mature/immature	terrific/dreadful
great/awful	respectful/ disrespectful	valuable/worthless
humane/inhumane	responsible/ irresponsible	wonderful/horrible
		worthy/unworthy

good/bad	should/shouldn't	deserve
right/wrong	must/must not	never/always
	have to	

Pure Observation

When we remove judgments of rightness and wrongness and stop blaming, what are we left with? We're left with what actually happened, without additional interpretations. This is *pure observation*. You might think of this as similar to the spiritual principle of "being the witness." We're simply observing. We then use our sensory information—what we see, hear, or sense by touch, smell, and/or taste—to describe the event. It's like what we might hear or see through an audio or video recording.

Here are some examples of changing a judgment (implying rightness or wrongness) into pure observation (without interpretation):

Judgment: "I feel *betrayed*."
Pure Observation: "You said you would take me to the dance, but now I've heard you're planning to go with Marcia."

Judgment: "He is *oversensitive*."
Pure Observation: "When I touched his arm, he jumped back about three feet."

Judgment: "That was *inappropriate*."
Pure Observation: "She questioned her boss's choice in the middle of the meeting."

Judgment: "They're *destroying* the planet."
Pure Observation: "I'm thinking about all the forests that are getting clear cut."

Judgment: "They *never* arrive on time."
Pure Observation: "I'm remembering the last three occasions

when they arrived thirty minutes after the time we agreed upon."

Judgment: "I'm *stupid*."
Pure Observation: "I've been told not to do that before, but I just did it again."

Judgment: "She *insulted* me."
Pure Observation: "She told me I have the intelligence of a three-year-old."

In the last example, the observation references a spoken judgment. Assuming that these words were actually uttered, the statement is still a pure observation. No additional interpretation of rightness or wrongness has been added. If you were to play a recording of the interaction, these are the words you would hear.

The examples above could have been spoken out loud or simply experienced as thoughts. Either way, they reflect our consciousness. Each time we think or speak in these ways, we reinforce that consciousness. Judgments reinforce our 3D consciousness of "me versus you" or "us versus them." Pure observation creates new neural pathways and habits for a higher consciousness.

A pure observation is usually quite short. Many of us think it's necessary to tell the whole story, blow by blow, in order to be understood. In the heart path, it's understood that recounting everything that occurs is neither necessary nor supportive for heart connection. Extra details tend to keep us in our mind. To support going into the heart, we pare down our description of the outer event to the essentials. We call this pared-down version *the stimulus*.

Yet what occurs is still important. We don't want to eliminate the outer event entirely. The event grounds our inner experience in our outer reality. When people express only their inner experience (e.g. "I feel sad" or "I feel elated") without sharing the stimulus, we often feel a sense of incompleteness and frustration in connecting with the person or understanding their experience. We need to know the *why* (what happened that stimulated the feeling), but we want to keep the *why* as brief as possible, so it doesn't keep us in our head. We want to stay focused on going into our heart.

Expressing the Stimulus

Identifying and expressing a concise stimulus is a conscious practice. This practice requires that we go inside ourselves, letting go of the details surrounding the event or our thoughts about it. Instead, we focus our awareness on the effect upon us of what has occurred and why we care about it. Doing so supports our self-connection and self-awareness.

Here are the steps for expressing a stimulus:

1. **Identify the one part of "the story" that has the most charge for you.** Most incidents snowball, leading to numerous parts that you're reacting to. Find the one incident among all the components that you're reacting to the most. This will be a specific moment in time when one specific thing happened.

2. **Describe what occurred without adding judgment or blame.** Limit the description to what would be recorded on a video or audio recording.

3. **Be succinct.** Simply state what happened, by whom, when it happened, and possibly where it happened. Do this in as few words as possible, optimally in a single phrase or sentence.

Telling the Story: "We love our home. We've been living here for twelve years. We've always been great tenants, doing extra things to maintain the place and never being late on rent. Now, right before Christmas, our landlord is kicking us out. He's decided he can make more money by selling the place. But there aren't any rentals available. The housing market here has gone crazy, with places selling for astronomical amounts. So all the owners want to sell instead of rent, and we're completely stuck with no place else to go. I asked the landlord if we could have more time to find a new place, but he said no. I can't believe it! After all we've done for him for all these years! And it's right before Christmas, with our kids coming to visit. I don't know what we're going to do. I just keep crying, and I can't sleep at night."

Expressing a Stimulus: "When I think about how our lease is ending in two weeks, and we can't find another place . . ."

A stimulus is usually a phrase rather than a complete sentence. It sets the stage for the next parts of the heart-path process, where we focus on what's been stimulated inside us by the outer event. This inner focus sets the heart path apart as a different orientation to life. It's also what supports our heart connection. We'll be learning about these next parts in the following chapters.

The Self-Judgment Stage

What often occurs at this point is "the light goes on," as people begin to recognize their own patterns of judging. This frequently gives rise to self-judgments, such as:

"I've been totally unaware."
"I've wasted so much time because I didn't understand this."
"I did it wrong in my past relationships."
"I'm going to say this wrong."

These self-judgments are frequently accompanied by feelings of discouragement or despair. I appreciate the frustration that people may experience when they realize their habits in the past or present don't support their spiritual life as much as they wish. Yet I see a different perspective. These kinds of self-judgments tell me that a person is "waking up." They're noticing their previously unconscious patterns, which is the first step toward change.

If you find yourself making self-judgments, be gentle with yourself. Later, we'll discuss how to mourn our past choices so that our pain can be healed. For now, consider your newfound awareness—and any accompanying self-judgment—as a sign of waking up, however painful that may be. As much as you're able, continue to learn the heart-path process. If you do, you'll learn to channel the energy of those self-judgments in different ways that support you to become the person you want to be.

One other thing that people frequently notice at this point is that shifting from judgment to pure observation alters their feeling about what's expressed. The message goes from being emotionally charged to neutral. However, Mary isn't suggesting that we stifle or suppress our energy. Instead, she's guiding us to redirect that energy for a more beneficial outcome. In the next steps of the heart path (which we cover in the following chapters), the energy that used to be carried in judgments is expressed through feelings. In doing so, we make a 180-degree turn with that energy. We're no longer projecting our energy outward. Instead, we are turning our energy inward where it can feed our healing and growth. I see this as calling our energy back to ourselves.

What Nonjudgment Isn't

I want to clear up a few misconceptions about nonjudgment. The first is that nonjudgment means to condone in a blanket fashion. This might be expressed as:

"It's all good."
"No problem."
"Don't worry, be happy."

Part of being human involves discernment between the things we're aligned with and those we're not. In the heart path, this discernment comes through feeling (rather than judgment). Feelings such as dislike, wariness, doubt, concern, aversion, horror, and so on are indicators that our inner divinity is not presently fulfilled. This is important information that we don't want to override with ideas that everything is fine. Connecting with our feelings is highly accurate and powerful for clarifying our "yes's" and our "no's" and for directing us to our next steps in supporting ourselves. How to genuinely identify our feelings is discussed in depth in the next chapter.

A second misperception is that letting go of labeling things as right or wrong is the same as passivity. In this line of thinking, people tend to fear that nonjudgment will lead to anarchy and the basest forms of human behavior taking over. Again, this is not what Mary is proposing. Mary's path empowers us to act from the heart. Such actions include our whole self because the heart is inclusive of the whole. Contrary to what people think, such actions are stronger and more durable than those that come from our mind.

> **MARY MAGDALENE:** This is not to say that you will never act, that you will be merely passive. It's that you wait to act until you are in union with God, and you let your action be directed by God. Then you are free, already free in God, and your action is God's play, however serious it may appear.
>
> *Mary Magdalene Beckons,* "The Great Freedom," p. 228

A third misunderstanding is to think of nonjudgment as meaning "Just accept whatever is happening." This concept shows up especially among spiritually oriented people who've been taught that to be spiritual is *not* to be affected by the experiences of life. This orientation may be expressed as:

"I shouldn't let this bother me."
"It's really a small thing."
"Everything is perfect just as it is."
"I should remain detached."
"I must accept this."

These approaches are often viewed as spiritually evolved, even saintly. But Mary is suggesting something different, related to the Feminine and Masculine parts of ourselves and our reality.[9]

According to Mary, we all (women *and* men) have both an inner Feminine and an inner Masculine aspect. Mary affirms that we need to honor and include both parts of ourself. However, our cultural programming has been heavily weighted toward the Masculine. Because of this, most of us are dominated by our Masculine side, and our Feminine side is underdeveloped. In fact, she says most of us no longer know our Feminine part. This is true of women as well as men. Mary is dedicated to changing this.

The examples above illustrate a classically Masculine approach to spirituality. This orientation can be a powerful spiritual practice, but it also comes with a risk. By choosing not to be involved in life experience, we may fall into *spiritual bypassing*. We may discount or deny parts of our reality—the Feminine part.

In the Feminine orientation, *all* experiences are important. Nothing is "small" or unnecessary. All experience is a form of God made incarnate. Our experience isn't a diversion from our spiritual path; it *is* the path—if we understand how to listen and make use of it. To ignore or override our experience is to bypass our spiritual guidance and its great gifts.

Mary teaches the Feminine path of opening to experience rather than bypassing it. In this path, our experience takes us into the heart, where we unite with our Masculine side. We are then restored to our wholeness of Masculine *and* Feminine, as well as our wholeness of union with God.

Practice

AWARENESS

1. **Noticing Judgment and Blame:** Practice noticing judgment and blame, whether made by yourself or another person. These judgments and blame might be expressed out loud, or they might be thoughts. Identify the specific words that imply rightness or wrongness, or point to someone being at fault. Do this to strengthen your awareness of judgment and blame, while refraining from judging those who are engaging in these patterns. Simply notice.

2. **Changing to Pure Observation:** Practice silently changing judgment and blame into pure observation. Notice how you feel after making this change.

JOURNALING

1. **Record Judgments and Blame:** Write down judgmental statements or blame that you've heard during the day. See if you can rewrite the statements so that they convey pure observations.

2. **Make a Pure Observation:** Describe an outer event that occurred in your life that day as a pure observation. Practice expressing this in as few words as possible while still including the essential *who*, *what*, *when*, and possibly, *where*.

SELF-COMPASSION

Practice being gentle and kind with yourself in learning this material. The patterns of judgment and blame can run deep. While Mary's teaching often leads to big "Aha!" moments and awakenings, it may also be challenging, especially at first. Hold these ideas and practices lightly, as something you're exploring, to see if they resonate for you. Notice if they work and if you like the results.

TWO

Grow Your Feeling Ability

MARY MAGDALENE: Emotions are a particularly human function. Many beings are highly developed in their mental powers, but emotions are a human gift. It is your strength, and even your calling as part of the universal plan, to be leaders in the emotional realm. Humans are still coming up to this calling and learning how to embrace and make use of the power of emotions.

Mary Magdalene Beckons,
"Loving Your Body, Sexuality, and Emotions," p. 33

In the last chapter, we focused on making a pure observation of an external event. Now we take the second step on the heart path, which requires shifting our focus to our inner world. We'll be homing in on what that outer event triggered inside of us. To do that, we will tune in to our feelings—the highway to our inner world.

In this book I'm defining feelings as two things: emotions and physical sensations. Emotions are affective states, such as fear, sadness, anger, and happiness. Physical sensations are visceral, such as feeling tense, hot, or jittery. These two arenas—emotions and physical sensations—often overlap or occur simultaneously.

For example, when you feel scared, you may also feel sweaty. Either arena (emotions or physical sensations) can be used as entryways into our inner experience—what's happening inside.

Feelings are natural. If you've spent time around a baby or a young child, you'll notice they are quite vocal and expressive of their feelings. They cry when they feel disturbed or afraid. They smile, gurgle, and laugh when they're happy. They wave their arms and legs when they're excited. They hit, kick, and scream when they're angry. But somewhere along the line, many of us were trained to suppress our feelings. Usually, this happened at a young age. Our parents or caregivers, siblings, or friends gave us the message that it wasn't OK to express certain feelings.

Frequently, there's a gender bias to this training. Boys who display fear or sorrow are denounced as "sissies," "crybabies," or "scaredy cats." Girls who express anger are stigmatized as "unladylike." But in many cases, all feelings (other than happiness) are painted as bad or unacceptable. Through such messages, and the rewards or punishments that accompany them, children learn: *I won't be loved or accepted if I express what I'm feeling.*

Most parents aren't aware that they're instilling these messages, nor are they aware of the alternatives. However, Mary doesn't see this social conditioning as necessary and normal or "just the way we teach children to behave." From her point of view, training people to disconnect from their emotions is part of the indoctrination into the power structures of our third-dimensional world, a practice that has far-reaching consequences.

MARY MAGDALENE: Your capacity for feeling . . . has been intentionally shut down in you to make you easy to control. Even as very young children, most of you received messages that told you feelings were bad or forbidden if you wanted to be loved and accepted. Often you received these messages from parents who actually loved you and meant to support you, but they were just passing on the messages and training they'd received . . . .

Now I and others—many others—are suggesting to you a whole different course. And it is founded in feeling and awakening the heart on the basis of feeling. This is the platform that will reconnect you to the entire kingdom of God. Would you like this? Do you believe it's possible?

Mary Magdalene Beckons, "Join the River of Love," pp 277-278

Mary is calling us to reclaim our connection to ourselves and to God through our feeling capacity. In doing so we recover our wholeness and our power to be who we came here to be.

Common Beliefs about Feelings

MARY MAGDALENE: Much maligning has been done in relationship to the emotional body. You might say that it's gotten a lot of "bad press." . . . Many have taught you to deny and suppress

> your emotions because, then, you are cut off from your power and are easy to control. It is essential that you reconnect with your emotions and feelings, because these are essential pathways of connection to your heart.
>
> *Mary Magdalene Beckons,*
> "Loving Your Body, Sexuality, and Emotions," p. 33

Many of us are convinced that feelings are harmful or destructive. This particularly applies to painful feelings, such as anger, hurt, sadness, or fear. Here are some common beliefs people hold about feelings:

If I open to painful feelings, I'm going to experience the pain even more strongly—perhaps so strongly that I won't be able to handle it and will be overwhelmed.

If I open to painful feelings, I'm going to get stuck in the pain, like a hole I may never get out of.

If I express my painful feelings to others, I may get hurt.

If I express my painful feelings to others, I may lose love or friendship.

If others have painful feelings, I may get hurt.

All of these beliefs equate emotions with being unsafe—physically or emotionally.

Because of our beliefs equating painful feelings with danger, as well as our past experiences of actual pain, many of us avoid painful feelings at all costs. If avoidance is impossible, we escape the pain as quickly as possible. Mary Magdalene recommends a very different approach. She asserts that our feelings, including our painful feelings, are of great help to us. They're our friends. Rather than avoid them, she tells us to receive them and open ourselves to them, which takes us to our heart. Most of us have never learned this process, so Mary is our guide.

For Mary, feelings comprise a communication system for telling us what's going on within ourselves. Think of it as your inner GPS or guidance system. A feeling alerts you that something is going on that you need to be aware of. Feelings are also a highly accurate guide for discovering what that inner "something" is, so you can attend to it. I see that inner "something" as the pot of gold at the end of the rainbow. If you don't heed your feelings, you will miss the signals to care for yourself, and you won't make it to the pot of gold.

For those who are worried about getting stuck in painful feelings, here's the good news: once your feelings have guided you to your inner work, they resolve into peace. If they don't resolve, it's a sign that you're not there yet. Perhaps a deeper issue has been uncovered that can now be addressed. Or perhaps you're dealing with a big event, such as the death of a loved one, and it will take time for a full healing. Even so, you'll notice a strengthening of your peace and a lessening of the pain as a result of the heart-path process. If you continue to engage the heart-path process over time, you'll eventually arrive at a full sense of peace and resolution.

The Gift of Pain

MARY MAGDALENE: When you have pain, it is telling you that there is some way that you have closed off from God. If you only seek to make the pain go away, then you will not receive the help you are being given for you to change, heal, and grow. Most of your responses to pain are about making it go away—taking a medicine or drug, numbing yourself with distractions, diverting yourself by blaming others or some situation, or trying to "fix" it so that you don't have to feel the pain. It's not that you have to stay in the pain. But if you just try to get rid of the pain, you won't receive the benefit.

Mary Magdalene Beckons, "Responding to Pain," p. 45

Mary says that pain always has a gift for us that we need to receive. She's not saying, "Therefore, try to be in pain as much as you can." She's not a martyr. And she fully acknowledges that pain is painful. What she *is* saying is this: "When you feel pain, it's for an important purpose. Make use of it."

The purpose of pain is to help us to heal and grow spiritually. Pain increases our capacity for love.

MARY MAGDALENE: Pain actually grows your heart. It deepens you, makes you more compassionate, more open. It's like the Grand Canyon, which was formed by the river wearing away the rock. The process brought out the beauty that was hidden before, that was only there in potential. And so it is with pain.

It's part of the process of life at the third-dimensional level; it serves us, yet it is not necessarily easy to go through.

When you go through pain and keep your heart open, your capacity to receive love grows and is refined, and you are transformed.

Mary Magdalene Beckons, "The Two Faces of God," p. 138

Over the years of supporting people spiritually, many have asked me how they can receive their own guidance. Mary is showing us how to do just that—through following our feelings. When people understand and make use of their feelings as a form of guidance, they're often amazed at how their feelings lead them to exactly what they need. After witnessing this process so many times, I've become convinced that our feelings are our most reliable form of guidance, as well as our most accessible.

Building Your "Feeling Muscle"

As we release our old patterns of avoiding feelings, and replace those patterns with new practices of recognizing and opening to feelings, we're building our "feeling muscle." Like developing any muscle, this takes practice. How do we do this? There are a number of ways.

The first way of building your ability to feel is to use your intention. Set the intention that you will become aware of what you're feeling and that you'll open to those feelings. Intention is extremely powerful. Just intending alone can have amazing results.

The second great help in connecting with feelings is your body. As discussed earlier, physical sensations are part of our feeling system. Use your somatic experiences as signals. You might have a feeling of tightness in your shoulders that tells you you're feeling stressed. Butterflies in your stomach let you know you're nervous. Heat in your face often points to anger or embarrassment. These are examples of using your body as a guide to what you're feeling.

You can also make use of your mind. Begin with a simple model, which I call the *four primary feelings*. Here, feelings are divided into four general categories: happy, sad, angry, and afraid. (If it's easier to remember, you can use these four rhyming words: glad, sad, mad, and "frad.") When you're not sure what you're feeling, use the process of elimination. Identify which of the four feeling categories you're *not* experiencing, and soon only one will remain. That category will tell you, in a general way, what you're feeling. Then you can fine tune your feelings from there.

Another valuable tool in developing your ability to feel is the list of feeling words shown in *Mary Magdalene Beckons*.[10] Naming your feelings helps you identify them. It also leads to a greater awareness of the nuances and subtle differences amongst various feelings. You can use the process of elimination with these lists too. Scan through the list. Eventually, one or more words will pop out as accurate descriptors of your experience.

Joyful Feelings

AFFECTIONATE
compassionate
friendly
loving
open-hearted
sympathetic
tender
warm

ENGAGED
absorbed
alert
curious
engrossed
enchanted
entranced
fascinated
interested
intrigued
involved
spellbound
stimulated

HOPEFUL
expectant
encouraged
optimistic

JOYFUL
amused
delighted
glad
happy
jubilant
pleased
tickled

EXCITED
amazed
animated
ardent
aroused
astonished
dazzled
eager
energetic
enthusiastic
giddy
invigorated
lively
passionate
surprised
vibrant

GRATEFUL
appreciative
moved
thankful
touched

INSPIRED
amazed
awed
wonder

CONFIDENT
empowered
open
proud
safe
secure

EXHILARATED
blissful
ecstatic
elated
enthralled
exuberant
radiant
rapturous
thrilled

PEACEFUL
calm
clearheaded
comfortable
centered
content
equanimous
fulfilled
mellow
quiet
relaxed
relieved
satisfied
serene
still
tranquil
trusting

REFRESHED
enlivened
rejuvenated
renewed
rested
restored
revived

This chart is based upon the Feelings Inventory from the Center for Nonviolent Communication.
© 2005 by Center for Nonviolent Communication, www.cnvc.org.

Painful Feelings

FATIGUE
beat
burnt out
depleted
exhausted
lethargic
listless
sleepy
tired
weary
worn out

ANNOYED
Aggravated
dismayed
disgruntled
displeased
exasperated
frustrated
impatient
irritated
irked

ANGRY
enraged
furious
incensed
indignant
irate
livid
outraged
resentful

AVERSION
animosity
appalled
contempt
disgusted
dislike
hate
horrified
hostile
repulsed

CONFUSED
ambivalent
baffled
bewildered
dazed
hesitant
lost
mystified
perplexed
puzzled
torn

VULNERABLE
fragile
guarded
helpless
insecure
leery
reserved
sensitive
shaky

DISCONNECTED
alienated
aloof
apathetic
bored
cold
detached
distant
distracted
indifferent
numb
removed
uninterested
withdrawn

EMBARRASSED
ashamed
chagrined
flustered
guilty
mortified
self-conscious

YEARNING
envious
jealous
longing
nostalgic
pining
wistful

Painful Feelings *(continued)*

AFRAID
apprehensive
dread
foreboding
frightened
mistrustful
panicked
petrified
scared
suspicious
terrified
wary
worried

TENSE
anxious
cranky
distressed
distraught
edgy
fidgety
frazzled
irritable
jittery
nervous
overwhelmed
restless
stressed out

SAD
depressed
dejected
despair
despondent
disappointed
discouraged
disheartened
forlorn
gloomy
heavy hearted
hopeless
melancholy
unhappy
wretched

PAIN
agony
anguished
bereaved
devastated
grief
heartbroken
hurt
lonely
miserable
regretful
remorseful

DISQUIET
agitated
alarmed
discombobulated
disconcerted
disturbed
perturbed
rattled
restless
shocked
startled
surprised
troubled
turbulent
turmoil
uncomfortable
uneasy
unnerved
unsettled
upset

This chart is based upon the Feelings Inventory from the Center for Nonviolent Communication.
© 2005 by Center for Nonviolent Communication, www.cnvc.org.

Feelings are often described as positive or negative. This is not how Mary views feelings. She asserts that *all* feelings are valuable and important. In this sense, they're all positive. You'll notice that the feeling lists are labeled as "joyful feelings" and "painful feelings" (rather than "positive feelings" and "negative feelings"). I recommend this shift into describing feelings as joyful or painful rather than judging feelings as good or bad.

Opening to Feelings

> **MARY MAGDALENE:** Feeling your emotions does not mean reacting to them or acting upon them. It means opening fully to them. It's like a woman receiving her lover. It's about receiving them and fully being with them. Perhaps you might think of a mother holding a crying child, not trying to talk to the child or fix the problem, but just holding the child and feeling with the child, helping the child to center and be with the pain. The feelings themselves lead us to the healing we require and through to the other side. We can trust that process.
>
> *Mary Magdalene Beckons,*
> "Loving Your Body, Sexuality, and Emotions," p. 34

If you're used to avoiding feelings, learning to open to them can feel uncomfortable. You might tell yourself that you "should" be doing something—most likely something to get rid of the pain. But feeling is primarily about *being* rather than *doing*. Here's another description from Mary of the experience of opening to feeling:

> **MARY MAGDALENE:** The dark night of the soul is about facing your fear and pain and going into it rather than avoiding it.
>
> What happens when you do that? It is not what you fear. There is an initial period in which you feel your fear, feel your pain, whatever it is. There is often a feeling of expansion with this, since you usually have shrunk back or contracted away from the pain or fear. There is a sense of relaxing and opening as your feeling nature expands into your whole experience. At some point, often sooner than you would expect, a shift happens. At that point, your experience changes to one of trust and peace, perhaps a sense of being carried—as in carried by a river rather than fighting against the current.
>
> What has happened is that you have connected with the beings of light that are there to support you, to carry you. The pain may or may not go away, but your experience of it is different because you are in the light. The light is stronger—and you are more attracted to it—than your pain. You have entered the River of Light, and it is now cleansing and guiding you.
>
> *Mary Magdalene Beckons,*
"The Dark Night of the Soul," pp. 59-60

There's a term in Nonviolent Communication (NVC) that I've found to be very helpful in the process of opening to pain. They refer to opening to any kind of painful feeling as *mourning*. Most of us think of mourning in a narrower sense, referring to a time of feeling sadness after a loss. In this expanded usage, mourning is the process of opening to all painful feelings. Thus, it includes not only sadness but also fear, anger, regret, and all other forms of pain.

Naming the process of opening to any kind of pain as "mourning" reinforces the necessity to feel the full spectrum of pain, so we can live from the heart. Through mourning all of our painful feelings, we learn to value them, to make space and time to feel them, and to let them do their essential work of healing, guiding, and growing us.

There's an art to mourning. On the one hand, you want to fully allow and experience your pain. On the other hand, you also want to remain attentive to when your mourning is complete and has fulfilled its purpose. To continue to focus on the pain beyond that point is counterproductive. If someone goes on and on about their pain, often repeating what they've already expressed, they're usually not allowing themselves to feel. They're coming from their mind and describing their pain, rather than letting themselves "drop down" into the experience of feeling it.

When we let ourselves feel our pain fully, it always resolves. At some point there's a subtle relaxation and letting go, along with a sense of "enoughness." It's like a child who's been allowed to cry fully and then is done. This is the place of *resolution for now*. Now there's freed-up energy for the next step in the heart path—connecting our feelings to our inner divinity, which leads us to true peace.

The counterpart to mourning is *celebrating*. Our joyful feelings are for celebration. Again, by naming our experience of joy as "celebrating," we're helped to fully open to our feelings. In doing so, we more fully experience our aliveness and receive the gifts of feeling.

In actuality, we're always either mourning or celebrating because we're always having some kind of feeling. Even if we aren't aware of feeling anything, we're still having feelings. We might be feeling calm, peaceful, or content, or perhaps we're feeling numb.

As we develop our skill of noticing and identifying feelings, a whole world of richness and aliveness opens to us.

Two Ways

Mary gives us two different techniques for responding to pain. The first one is the simpler form, which I call *pure surrender*. This is to simply open to the pain and allow ourself to fully experience it. As we do this, Mary tells us to call on God to guide and direct us to whatever is needed in the situation.

The second technique involves using our feelings to connect with their deeper sources within ourselves. This approach is discussed in chapter three.

When we surrender, we use the strength of our inner Feminine, our receptive side, to respond to the situation that is evoking feelings. This applies to everyone, men and women, since we all have an inner Feminine and Masculine. Mary describes this process here:

> **MARY MAGDALENE:** When you feel pain, turn to God.... Ask God to help you. Ask all your angels, Spirit helpers, and beings of light you're connected to, to help you. Ask them to work with the situation. Ask them to connect with the Christ consciousness of the other people involved and to help you connect with Christ consciousness. Ask your Spirit helpers to connect with the Spirit helpers of any other beings involved. Ask for the highest outcome for all involved. Ask that, "Thy will be done,"

> which is a way of inviting the highest beings to be involved for the good of all. Ask that Christ consciousness be infused into the situation and that it alter the events in whatever way is for the best for all. Ask until you feel yourself let go. That is surrender. You will know it because you come to peace.
>
> *Mary Magdalene Beckons*, "Responding to Pain," p. 46

Many of us have been taught not to ask for help. We think we should be strong and able to handle things on our own and that asking for help is imposing on others. Mary is saying just the opposite. The more we ask for help, the more we open ourselves to God and the more God can help us.

If you're like me, this isn't easy. I've habituated myself to not asking for help. I have to remind myself (or others need to remind me) that it's not only possible but advisable to ask for help. This is where support from friends can be invaluable.

However, frequently when we're in pain and we ask friends for support, they offer things that reinforce our avoidance mechanisms. They might analyze what's occurred with questions such as, "When did this start?", "How many times has this happened?", or "Is this your pattern to be in this situation?" These analytical responses tend to keep us in our head.

Another common response is to offer solutions to "fix" the problem. Or our friends may immediately shift the focus to themselves and talk about similar incidents in their own life.

In all these responses, people are usually doing their best to help. But in reality these approaches take us away from the heart process. So we need to use discernment about who we turn to when we're in pain. It's best to find someone, or something, that will truly support you in opening to your pain. Whether it's a friend, a therapist, a religious support person, or another human helper, you may need to guide them in giving you the kind of support you want.

You can begin by thanking them for wanting to help you. Then describe what would support you the most. You may need someone to reflect back the feelings you're having so that you can fully connect with them. You can let the person know that you're not ready for solutions to the problem. Right now you just need to connect with your feelings.

You can always ask for help from God, by whatever name or form that you prefer. You may relate to God as Spirit, Source, Higher Power, Mother-Father God, or by some other designation or metaphor. You can also ask for help from your higher self, angels, spirit guides, or through Christ consciousness. Whatever form is real for you, that's what or who you can turn to.

Some people have the idea that asking God or higher beings for help isn't necessary. They think these elevated beings already know what's going on with us and, therefore, will automatically give us whatever we need. Mary clarifies that especially with these beings, asking for their help is both necessary and important. Higher beings are extremely conscious of respecting our free will. They wait for us to ask before they intervene on our behalf because they don't want to interfere with our soul process and choices. For our part, the process of asking makes us more available to receive.

The second process Mary gives for opening to feelings is more structured. For most people this second process is easier than pure surrender. In this approach we use our feelings to connect with their deeper source within ourselves, which she calls our *inner divine qualities*. In my work I've found this approach to be most valuable for healing and growth. As mentioned above, we will explore this second process in depth in chapter three.

Eventually, as we gain skill in opening to feelings, the two paths merge. The second way becomes natural, like riding a bike, and it, too, becomes a form of surrender.

Non-Feelings

We often say, "I feel . . .," but what follows frequently isn't what we're defining as a feeling. Rather it's a thought, usually a judgmental thought. I call this a *non-feeling*. Here are some examples:

"I FEEL LIKE . . ." OR "I FEEL THAT . . ."

Non-Feeling: "*I feel like* this course is extremely valuable."
Feeling: "I feel excited about taking this course."

Non-Feeling: "*I feel that* was a terrible thing to say."
Feeling: "I feel disturbed about what was said."

In these non-feelings, the focus is external and includes a judgment of good/bad or right/wrong. When we change the statement into a feeling, our focus makes a U-turn back to ourself.

PRONOUNS

Non-Feeling: "*I feel she* is so confused about what's going on."
Feeling: "I feel concerned when I talk to her because each time her story changes."

Non-Feeling: *I feel it* is damaging.
Feeling: I feel worried about it.

Again, the non-feeling is really a thought about something external that expresses a judgment.

ACTIONS OF OTHERS

Non-Feeling: "*I feel intimidated.*"
Feeling: "I feel scared."

Non-Feeling: "*I feel ignored.*"
Feeling: "I feel frustrated."

Non-Feeling: "*I feel rejected.*"
Feeling: "I feel lonely."

These non-feelings describe actions that another person is taking. When we translate them into feelings, we express the emotions or bodily sensations that we're experiencing.

SELF-JUDGMENTS

Non-Feeling: "*I feel stupid.*"
Feeling: "I feel exasperated."

Non-Feeling: "*I feel worthless.*"
Feeling: "I feel sad."

Non-Feeling: "*I feel important.*"
Feeling: "I feel exuberant."

With self-judgments, we make ourselves the "other" as we assume the position of judge. Self-judgments usually carry a deep sense of criticism, blame, and shame. Replacing self-judgments with feelings returns us to a sense of wholeness, setting us on a course of self-acceptance and self-love while empowering us to change.

Non-feelings focus on the other and what's outside ourselves while feelings redirect our focus to what's happening with us on the inside. Non-feelings separate us from others and ourselves, with an accompanying sense of harshness; feelings open us to our vulnerability and help us become softer. Non-feelings keep us in our head while feelings lead us to our heart. Most importantly, feelings empower us to heal and grow rather than simply cope with life's events. They take us to Source.

Hybrid Feelings

There are four feelings that I call *hybrid feelings*: anger, shame, guilt, and depression. Hybrid feelings are a mixture of judgments and feelings.

The problem with hybrid feelings is that we get stuck in them. Pure feelings are always changing, if we allow them to be fully felt. When we mix feelings with judgments, the judgments hold the feelings in place, so they don't resolve.

The way to get unstuck is to separate the judgment from the deeper or truer emotion. This leads to the underlying feeling, which will be different from the hybrid feeling (anger, shame, guilt, or depression). Here's an example with reference to anger:

Hybrid Feeling (spoken with anger): "These drivers are *idiots!*"

In this example the feeling of anger is combined with the judgment of the other drivers as idiots. When we set the judgment aside, the anger settles into a different underlying emotion:

Underlying Feeling: "When that driver pulled into my lane with no warning, I felt afraid."

Now the hybrid emotion of anger has given way to the deeper emotion of fear. Dropping down into this purer emotion releases the judgment. With that our stuck energy is released and can now help us move into our heart.

When we're experiencing hybrid emotions (anger, guilt, shame, or depression), writing down the judgments we're having can help bring them to consciousness, so we can set them aside. Another way to bring our judgments into awareness is to say them out loud, perhaps in a dramatic way. Once we've identified and set aside our judgments (at least for the moment), the deeper feeling, which is different from the initial hybrid emotion, emerges.

Freeing the Heart

In closing this chapter on feeling, I want to offer one of my favorite excerpts from *Mary Magdalene Beckons*, where Mary underscores the importance of growing in feeling.

> **MARY MAGDALENE:** I call you to be a warrior for God and for peace. And this begins within yourself, by breaking free of the shackles that have been placed on your ability to feel and connect with your heart . . . . You can support the old system of control and subservience by shutting down your feeling nature and your connection to God, or you can support the path of freedom by

> engaging your feeling and loving connection to God through your heart. In every moment, you have a choice, and the choice happens through feeling.
>
> *Mary Magdalene Beckons*, "Join the River of Love," p. 279

Practice

AWARENESS

Once per day, read the list of feelings out loud. As you read each feeling, open to the energy communicated through the particular word and the feeling-quality it evokes. Notice all the different feelings that are possible to experience.

JOURNALING

1. **Avoiding Feeling:** Write down the things you do, or have done in the past, to avoid feeling. Record things you notice others doing to avoid feeling.

2. **Feelings Experienced:** Notice and record the feelings you have each day. Connect each feeling with a concise description of the situation that stimulated the feeling.

THREE

Connect to Your Inner Divinity

MARY MAGDALENE: Emotions are always motivated by beautiful qualities, what I would call divine aspects of ourselves. By letting ourselves fully feel and experience our emotions, we will be led to these divine aspects.

Mary Magdalene Beckons,
"Loving Your Body, Sexuality, and Emotions," p. 34

We are now ready to explore what our feelings are pointing to—our inner divinity. Of all the parts of the heart-path process, this portion is usually the most unfamiliar and, therefore, the most challenging. We generally haven't been taught about our inner divinity, nor have we been supported in connecting with it. Because of our lack of development in this area, people often "lose the trail" at this point—they stop after connecting with their feelings and thus don't receive the sweetest fruits of the heart-path process.

I can't emphasize it enough: keep going! Linking your feelings to your inner divinity is the *most important part* of the heart path. This is what restores us to our wholeness. It may take a conscious intention (or support from others) to continue with this step. But the deep resolution and peace it brings makes it well worth the extra attention required.

Purpose of Feelings

Understanding Inner Divinity

Mary tells us that our inner divinity is made up of beautiful qualities, which she calls our *inner divine qualities*. These qualities are all the different aspects that collectively make up the divine part of us—something like our divine DNA. All human beings experience these inner divine qualities as part of being human.

Inner Divine Qualities

CONNECTION
acceptance
affection
appreciation
belonging
cooperation
communication
closeness
community
companionship
compassion
consideration
consistency
empathy
inclusion
intimacy
love
mutuality
nurturing
respect
safety
security
stability
support
to know and
  be known
to see and be seen
to understand and
  be understood
trust
warmth

PHYSICAL WELL-BEING
air
food
movement/exercise
rest/sleep
sexual expression
safety
shelter
touch
water

HONESTY
authenticity
integrity
presence

PLAY
joy
humor

PEACE
beauty
communion
ease
equality
harmony
inspiration
order

MEANING
awareness
celebration of life
challenge
clarity
competence
consciousness
contribution
creativity
discovery
efficacy
effectiveness
growth
hope
learning
mourning
participation
purpose
self-expression
stimulation
to matter
understanding

AUTONOMY
choice
freedom
independence
space
spontaneity

This chart is drawn from the Needs Inventory by the Center for Nonviolent Communication.
© 2005 by Center for Nonviolent Communication, www.cnvc.org.

Our inner divine qualities are beautiful because they describe God's beauty. Even when we're experiencing painful feelings, those feelings are emanating from a beautiful part of ourselves, our God part. Knowing that our inner divine qualities are always beautiful can be a guide for evaluating whether we've accurately identified an inner divine quality. Ask yourself: *Is this something beautiful that lives inside me?*

Inner divine qualities make up the center or core of who we are. They are what's truly motivating us all the time, whether we're aware of it or not. When we connect with this deep part of ourselves, we connect with what's alive and driving us at the very essence of our being.

Everyone's soul inherently "knows" these qualities of God. Even when an inner divine quality is not currently fulfilled or hasn't been fulfilled for a long time, the fact that we miss or seek it shows that we know what it is to have it. We can't miss what we haven't once known, had, or possessed.

Another hallmark of inner divine qualities is that they're universal. We all share the same inner divine qualities. We also share the same drives to fulfill these essential parts of ourselves. This inner sameness connects us with all other humans at a profound level—a spiritual level. You could even say it connects us at a God level.

Outer Events Don't Cause Our Feelings

MARY MAGDALENE: If you are in pain, it's not because of what someone else has done to you. It's because you have lost your connection with God. If you understand this, pain is an avenue of connection with God, and it will lead you to freedom, peace, and joy.

Mary Magdalene Beckons, "Opening the Heart," p. 198-199

The conventional point of view is that feelings are caused by the events and circumstances of life. Mary agrees that there's a relationship between life events and feelings, but she says the relationship is different than most of us think. **The effect of outer events—whatever happened—is to cause our inner divine qualities to either be fulfilled or not fulfilled.** Then, as an indicator that something is going on with one of our inner divine qualities, a feeling arises. If the inner divine quality is fulfilled by the outer event, the feeling that arises is joyful. If the inner divine quality is not fulfilled by the outer event, the feeling that arises is painful.

Here's an example:

Outer Event/Stimulus: "My dog got hit by a car."

Effect on Inner Divine Qualities: "My inner divine qualities of *protection* (of a loved one) and *well-being* (of a loved one) are not fulfilled."

Feelings that Arise: "I feel *upset* and *sad*."

Source of Our Feelings

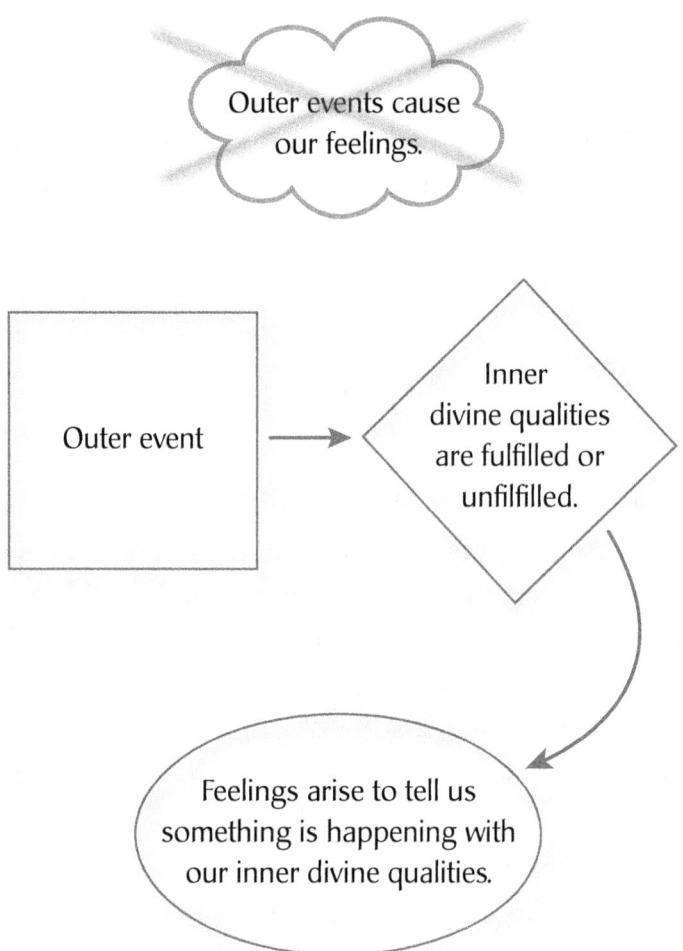

The stimulus or outer event causes the person's inner divine qualities of protection (of a loved one) and well-being (in regard to a loved one) to be unfulfilled. The feelings (being upset and sad) let the person know that their inner divine qualities need tending.

Why is this important? If our feelings are caused by outer events, we usually have little power over those events. However, if our feelings are caused by our inner divine qualities being fulfilled or unfulfilled, that is something we have power over. We can take steps to change what's going on so that our unfulfilled inner divine qualities become fulfilled. If they're already fulfilled (which joyful feelings would indicate), we can celebrate that fulfillment.

This change—from seeing events as the cause of our feelings, to seeing inner divine qualities as the cause—shifts us out of "victim" consciousness. We become a person with choices, a creator. We have the power to heal and change within ourselves.

This shift also alters our relationship to our feelings. Feelings, including painful feelings, become valuable rather than unwanted things to be gotten rid of. They're a source of information and a navigator of our inner world, helping us reap our inner riches.

Which Inner Divine Quality Needs Attention?

While feelings call out to our awareness, inner divine qualities are silent. That's why we need feelings as signals, to alert and call attention to our inner divine qualities and what's happening with them. Feelings then help us figure out which inner divine quality needs tending. The heart path shows us how to follow our feelings to locate the specific inner divine quality that needs our attention. Here are the steps for doing that:

1. **Identify the feeling.** By starting with your feeling rather than the outer event, you direct your focus toward yourself and your inner world.

2. **Connect the feeling to a stimulus (outer event).** At what specific point in time did the feeling begin? In other words, in the previous moment you didn't have the feeling, but now you do. What occurred at the moment the feeling arose?

   Keep the description of the stimulus as brief as possible to support your focus on yourself and your inner world. But do include the essentials of what has occurred because that grounds the event in the context of your life.

3. **Match the feeling to an inner divine quality.** If the feeling is painful, ask yourself:

   Which inner divine quality is this feeling pointing to that's not fulfilled by this event? What am I longing for in this circumstance?

   If the feeling is joyful, ask:

   Which inner divine quality is this feeling pointing to that is fulfilled by this event?

Identifying an Inner Divine Quality

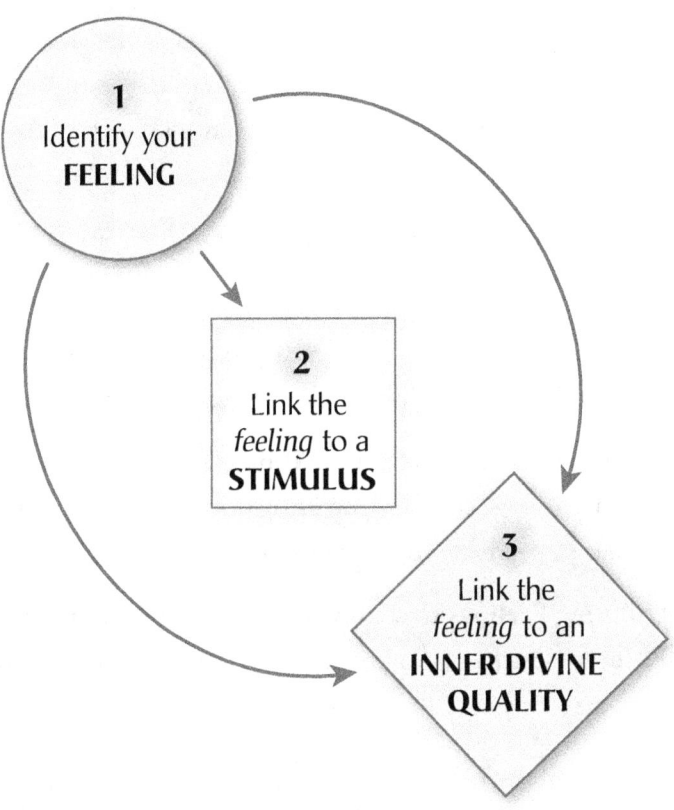

Ask yourself:
Which inner divine quality is this feeling pointing to that's fulfilled or not fulfilled?

Inner Divine Qualities Are Universal

> **MARY MAGDALENE:** All your feelings are ultimately rooted in your connection with God.
>
> Mary Magdalene Beckons, "Opening the Heart," p. 198

Our inner divine qualities always refer to universal qualities that we all share. They never refer to specific people or specific actions.

Attributing Feelings to Specific People and Actions: "When I see the garbage overflowing in the kitchen, I feel frustrated because I need *you* to *take the garbage out*."

Attributing Feelings to a Universal Inner Divine Quality: "When I see the garbage overflowing in the kitchen, I feel frustrated because I need *support*."

The first example doesn't refer to an inner divine quality. All humans don't share a need for "you" (a specific person) to "take the garbage out" (a specific action). The second example is universal. We all share a need for support.

Compare how you feel when you hear these two statements. In the first statement, the implication is that the other person has done something wrong. This tends to arouse defensiveness or resistance (or both!) in the other person.

The second statement tends to engender a more harmonious response. The speaker is only talking about themselves and what's going on with them on the inside. This kind of sharing of our inner life makes us vulnerable. In receiving that vulnerability, listeners are more likely to let their guard down. They're more likely to hear what's being said and to understand and care about the speaker's experience. This leads to a different response.

In the example above, I want to underscore that our ultimate form of support is in God. This quality of ultimate support by God lives inside of us all the time as our inner divinity. But life events can shock us out of our inner God-connection. (In the example above, the life event was the garbage overflowing.) Then it's like a circuit breaker, where the switch gets flipped because the circuit is overloaded. Our job as spiritual beings is to reconnect that circuit. Our feelings point us to the specific circuit (an inner divine quality) that got switched off. Then we have the power to reconnect it.

Crossing the Bridge to God

When referring to an inner divine quality, we want to describe it in its whole or full state. This applies even when our feelings are painful. Why? Because our inner divinity is never diminished, even though outer circumstances may cause us to lose touch with that beautiful, unceasing inner state.

The examples below illustrate the difference between referring to an inner divine quality as missing or absent versus describing it as existing (even though we may not be currently experiencing it). The first sentence links pain to what we don't have. The second sentence links the same pain to what we're longing for.

Focusing on what we don't have: "I feel hurt because *my need for respect wasn't met.*"
Focusing on what we want: "I feel hurt because *I want respect.*"

This may seem like splitting hairs, but the distinction is quite important. These two ways of thinking or speaking reinforce two very different forms of consciousness.

Focusing on not having the inner divine quality reinforces deficiency or lack. We're reinforcing our separation from God. This orientation tends to leave us stuck in our pain.

Describing the inner divine quality in its fullness keeps us focused on what we *do* want and are invoking. We leave behind our sense of deficiency as we reach for our wholeness in God. *This shift is the true healing.* As spiritual practitioners, we're affirming that God—in this instance, a particular quality of God—is always available to us. I picture this moment as crossing the bridge to God. From this land of wholeness, new forms of action can sprout.

Connecting to the fullness of an inner divine quality isn't the same as having faith in it being fulfilled. The experience of a fulfilled inner divine quality is tangible and real. Some part of us knows what it is to have the completeness we long for. We can't miss something unless we know what it is to have it. I've consistently seen people connect with this "place" inside themself, even when they didn't previously realize it existed.

To connect with that inner place, I tell people: "Go inside and find the place in yourself that knows the fullness of that inner divine quality."[11] You might experience a certain location in your body where that ever-full inner divine quality "lives." You might see that place or feel it viscerally. Perhaps you'll receive a message or an image from that place. Perhaps memories will surface of a time when that inner divine quality was fulfilled.

When you connect with that place within, let yourself merge with it as if you were immersing yourself in a pool of that inner divine quality in its fullness. Give yourself the experience of being filled up with the inner divine quality you're longing for.

If it's difficult for you to connect with that inner place of wholeness, it may mean you've been cut off from it for a long time. You may even be convinced that you can never have that quality for yourself. If that's the case, you may need to *imagine* having that inner divine quality fulfilled. Or imagine someone you know who has that inner divine quality fulfilled and then imagine having their inner experience.

Not being able to connect with the inner divine quality in its wholeness may also point to something else. You may not have found the quality yet that's at the root of your feelings. In this case when you try to connect with the always-full inner divine quality, you'll have new feelings or thoughts come up, possibly even judgments. This is valuable too. These feelings or thoughts provide further guidance, leading you to a different inner divine quality that's the true source of your feelings. Let whatever has surfaced point you to the currently emerging inner divine quality. Then engage the same process of locating and merging with that inner divine quality in its fullness.

Match the Feeling and the Inner Divine Quality

There's one more refinement relative to identifying the inner divine quality at the source of a particular situation. Make sure that the feeling and the inner divine quality align. Here are examples, illustrating the difference between a) feelings and inner divine qualities that don't match versus b) feelings and inner divine qualities that align:

> **Non-Matching Feeling and Inner Divine Quality:** "When you said my hat was ugly, I felt *hurt* because I need *freedom* to dress the way I want."

The feeling of being hurt and the inner divine quality of freedom don't match. Connecting them is based on a thought, such as: *Wearing this hat fulfills my inner divine quality of freedom (to wear whatever I choose)*. That thought may be true, but it doesn't pertain to the feeling of being hurt. If you let the feeling guide you, rather than your thoughts, you'll be led to a different inner divine quality, as illustrated below.

> **Matching Feeling and Inner Divine Quality:** "When you said my hat was ugly, I felt *hurt* because I need *kindness*."

Now the feeling (hurt) and the inner divine quality (kindness) match.

Here's an example of a different feeling that would match with the inner divine quality of freedom:

> **Different Feeling that Matches the Inner Divine Quality:** "When you told me not to speak during the movie, I felt *exasperated* because I need *freedom* to do as I please."

Exasperation and freedom go together, relative to the situation of being told not to speak during the movie.

Developing the ability to discern whether the feeling and inner divine quality match often takes time and practice, but eventually, the path of following feelings versus thoughts will become clear. Feelings are more trustworthy than thoughts. As you learn to let your feelings take the guiding role, your thoughts will naturally assume a supporting position of fleshing out the evidence for your feelings.

The Shift into Peace

> **MARY MAGDALENE:** Connecting with the source of your pain will bring about a shift. You will experience an opening, a peacefulness of connection with Source, with God, because you have connected with the root drive of union with the Divine.
>
> *Mary Magdalene Beckons,* "Opening the Heart," p. 198

When you've identified the inner divine quality at the root of a situation, you will experience a recognizable shift within your body. Most often, people describe this shift as "coming to peace." The sense of peace tells us: *I don't need to go any further. I'm there.* This shift is often accompanied by a sigh, as well as a visible release of tension, or a subtle "dropping" into the body. The stress of being disconnected from our inner divinity is being released. This is the primary sign that you've tapped into the true inner divine quality that's at the source of what's manifesting.

The beauty of this process is that becoming aware of the inner divine quality in a given circumstance is all we need to bring about our reconnection. The process is quite simple. Our awareness is like a divine beam of light, shining the luminosity of consciousness on the inner divine quality that we've disconnected from.

And voila! We're connected again. I've witnessed this process countless times. Each time is like a little miracle where someone reconnects with God.

Once you've reconnected with your inner divinity, give yourself space to experience that connection. Drop into the feeling of peace and wholeness. Don't go back to your thoughts because that will take you out of your heart and back to your mind.

Next Steps

At this point there are two different directions your heart may want to go. You might feel drawn to just be with the inner divine quality you've identified. I call this *cocooning* because it's an inward process. You're taking time to strengthen your connection to that inner divine quality and integrate it into your being. You may especially need this if you've been disconnected from that particular inner divine quality for a while.

Alternatively, you may feel energized and creative, ready to take action. This can occur right away (if you don't need a period of integration) or after your cocooning is complete. The process of moving into action after reconnecting with your inner divinity will be our focus in the next chapter.

MARY MAGDALENE: Feel your pain, feel it fully, without avoiding it by going to your judgmental thinking. Be with the feeling and let it reopen your heart. And when that is full, use your mind to connect with the source, the beautiful attribute or quality that you are longing for. Now you will be able to feel the depth of your longing for that God-quality, and that longing will return you to peace, harmony, and openness to Source.

Mary Magdalene Beckons, "Opening the Heart," p. 199

Practice

AWARENESS

Spend time each day reading through the list of inner divine qualities. Do this as a form of meditation. Speak each inner divine quality aloud, pausing after each one to notice how you experience that quality. Through doing this you'll familiarize yourself with the inner divine qualities, and they'll become more readily identifiable when you're working with a life situation.

JOURNALING

1. **Life Situations:** Think of a situation that generated a reaction in you. Then write down:

a. A concise description of the stimulus that occurred, without adding any extra judgment or blame to your description.

b. One or more feelings that were stimulated in you by this event.

c. The inner divine quality that each feeling is pointing to. Use the list of inner divine qualities to help you identify the inner divine quality involved.

2. **Deepening Understanding:** Each week, choose one inner divine quality to focus on. Each day, write down the ways that that particular inner divine quality was or wasn't fulfilled through the various events of the day.

FOUR

Ask for What You Want

MARY MAGDALENE: Asking is so important.
Mary Magdalene Beckons, "Responding to Pain," p. 47

Many of us have learned not to ask for what we want. As children we may have been told we were bad or a nuisance when we expressed our desires (partly due to our *way* of expressing them). This is the message that we internalized:

> *If I want to be loved, I shouldn't bother others with my requests. I should be "good," cooperative, and not make waves. I should go along with what others want.*

We then adapted by not expressing our desires. As adults this thinking deepened, often showing up in more sophisticated forms, such as:

> *Just accept the situation.*
> *It's selfish to pursue what I want.*
> *I should put others' needs before my own.*
> *It's better to give than to receive.*
> *It's spiritually evolved not to need anything.*

This type of thinking reinforces the idea: *I shouldn't ask for what I want.*

There are a number of problems with these beliefs. The first is that when we don't express what we want, we limit what's possible. Most of the time, others actually want to help us. Spirit wants to help us too. But we must do our part by revealing what we'd like.

A second problem with not asking for what we want is that we deprive others of the joy of giving to us. Giving and receiving are integral parts of engaging fully in life and relationships, but for most of us, receiving is more difficult than giving. In actuality, when we receive, we're also giving. We give a gift to others by allowing them to give to us. Our receiving completes a circle of connection and relationship between the giver and the receiver.

A third difficulty in not asking for what we want is that we're hiding parts of ourselves. This makes it harder for others to know who we really are and to get close to us. We can even lose touch with ourself through this hiding, to the point of not knowing what we really want. This kind of dissociation is often confused with being spiritual.

The habit of not expressing our desires can also lead to passivity, where we require others to read our mind and figure out what we want. We might even take such mind reading as a sign of caring or love: *If you really love me, you'll know what I want without my having to ask for it.*[12] However, most people aren't good at mind reading and experience this expectation as a burden. When we tell others what we want, we lighten their load, making it easier and often more joyful for them to give to us.

Respect Free Will

MARY MAGDALENE: We respect your free will. Even though we want to help you, we will not step in until you ask. We ask the same of you with others. Respect their free will.

Mary Magdalene Beckons, "Responding to Pain," p. 47

Many of us hold the belief that we must bring force to our requests in order to get the support we want. Even if we don't realize that we're exerting force, the effects are clearly felt by those on the receiving end.

A common expression of force is to raise your voice. Parents frequently do this with children, but it happens between adults too. It's a power strategy where volume is both a show of strength and a demand to get our way.

Another way of bringing force is to assume a position of authority. This is often expressed through delivering directives in a firm, commanding tone. In doing so we are telling others what they *must* do instead of asking them if they would do it. Here's an example:

"Get going right now!"

We also bring force when we imply that someone is obligated to do something because it's the "right" thing to do (or not doing it would be the "wrong" thing). This is sometimes called "guilt tripping." The most common judgmental words that are used for this kind of coercion are *should, must, have to, supposed to, deserve,* or *have a right to.* Here are some examples:

"You *should* go to your child's concert."
"You *have to* go to your child's concert."
"You're *supposed to* go to your child's concert."
"Your child *deserves* to have you come to their concert."
"Your child *has a right to* have a parent attend their concert."

Sometimes the use of force is overt, where there's an explicitly stated threat for non-compliance. Here are some examples:

"Eat your vegetables, or *you won't get dessert.*"
"Do what I say, or *you'll be sorry.*"
"Make this sales goal, or *you won't be eligible for a raise.*"
"Pay your taxes, or *you'll be fined.*"

Any time that force is used, we're making a demand. The test for a demand is not tone of voice—a "nice" tone doesn't rule out coercion. It's whether we'll accept a "no" in response to the request. If we won't accept "no," then we've made a demand.

Coercion and demands come at a cost. The most obvious is that it leads to resentment on the part of the receiver. That person's natural desire to help is quashed. Instead of freely giving, they will likely respond out of obligation, duty, or submission. Or they may respond in kind, bringing their own force in retaliation.

The second consequence of using force is that it results in separation. When we experience demands and coercion, our natural response is to distance ourselves and not associate with the person (or people) making the demand.

A third repercussion of demands and coercion is that we violate our own inner divine quality of respecting the autonomy of others and their free will. Mary Magdalene emphasizes that in the higher dimensions, beings are very aware and respectful of everyone's free will. Higher beings wait to act until they've been invited to do so. Or they ask for what they want but wait for an explicit "yes" before they proceed. Respect for free will is considered a sacred principle.

In the third dimension, it's often considered normal or even smart to bring force to get what we want. You could say it's "the name of the game" here, exemplified by the maxim: "Might makes right." Mary Magdalene's point of view is quite different. She says we're never truly fulfilled if our fulfilment comes at another's expense. True fulfillment ultimately rests in everyone's inner divine qualities being cared for and tended to. Mary calls this the *consciousness of inclusion,* a hallmark of fourth-dimensional consciousness. "Me versus you" has transformed into "me and you." This "me and you" consciousness is also a consciousness of abundance; there's enough for everyone's inner divine qualities to be fulfilled.

In the heart path, we replace force with requests. We ask for what we want with a willingness to accept a "no." There's no obligation for others to do what we ask, and we only want them to say "yes" if their agreement is authentic. This is a spiritual practice of trust in the abundance of the universe and, ultimately, trust in God's abundance. We're not limited to only one way of fulfilling our inner divine qualities. Nor are we dependent on one person to do a particular thing merely because we've thought up that solution at the moment. *There is always more than one way to fulfill our inner divine qualities.*[13] We have other options.

Helping Others

Many spiritually oriented people believe that part of our "job" as spiritual beings is to provide help and relief for others. Interestingly, the opposite is also held by some as a spiritual premise: "We should be detached and not involve ourselves with others' challenges or concerns." This kind of detachment is seen as a way of supporting other people's power to manifest: "They've created their reality, and they can change it if they want."

Here's what Mary Magdalene has to say about helping others:

> **MARY MAGDALENE:** If you want to help others, share it as your desire to help, to contribute to them, and ask them if they would like to receive that. And respect their choice . . . .
>
> This is a fine distinction, yet so important. Do not suppress yourself by suppressing your caring and concern for others. . . . Yet, these must be owned as your own desires, rather than your ideas of what others should or must do."
>
> *Mary Magdalene Beckons,*
> "The Consciousness of Inclusion," pp. 187-188

Mary is making four points here:

1. Don't suppress your desire to help others.

2. If you want to help someone, own that as *your* desire to contribute to them.

3. Respect other people's free will by *asking* whether they want to receive your help.

4. Respect other people's choice regarding whether they want your help.

In practical terms, this means asking others if they want your help *before giving it* and being willing to accept a "no" as a response. This includes asking if someone wants to hear your thoughts or advice, and *not* offering these if their response is "no."

> **MARY MAGDALENE:** If you feel concerned about another, express that, but own it as your concern. You do not know what is right for them. You can ask them to change, but do not cross the boundary into force, based on thinking that you know what they should be doing. Respect their choice, and then choose what you will do.
>
> Mary Magdalene Beckons,
> "The Consciousness of Inclusion," p. 187

This is a big shift for many people. It means not presuming that we know what's right for others. I think of this as "staying on our side of the street." We don't usurp other people's free choice or assume that we know better than they do regarding what they should do.

Skills for Making Requests

1. **Begin by sharing the feelings and inner divine qualities that are motivating your request.** This helps the other person understand why you're making the request. It also helps them connect with you from their heart.

2. **Express your request in the form of a question.**

   "Would you . . .?"

   This reinforces for you and the other person that you're respecting the other's free will and that you are open to receiving a "no."

3. **Request a concrete action.** Specify the concrete actions that will fulfill your inner divine quality. This makes it easier for the other person to give to you.

   Don't request feelings, as these can't be mandated. Don't request inner divine qualities because we all have different ideas of what would fulfill someone else's inner divine qualities. Don't request vague concepts since these are open to numerous interpretations.

   > **Requesting a Feeling:** "I just want you to *be happy*."
   > **Requesting a Concrete Action:** "Could we talk about what would make you happy?"

Requesting an Inner Divine Quality: "Would you *support me* while I'm going through this?"

Requesting a Concrete Action: "Would you call me once a week while I'm going through this and ask me how I'm doing?"

Vague Request: "Please *be on time.*"

Requesting a Concrete Action: "Can you arrive by 3:20?"

4. **Request what you *do* want, not what you *don't* want.** Making a request in the negative ("I don't want...") is a vague request. You're not clarifying what you *do* want and are, thereby, reducing the likelihood of receiving it.

    Negative Request: "I *don't* want you going out with your friends after school." (The person may respond by doing something else after school, such as going to the library.)

    Positive Request: "I'd like you to come directly home after school."

    In addition to being vague, negative requests are often heard as criticisms. This also undermines the likelihood of getting the cooperation you'd like.

5. **A "no" isn't a rejection or the end of the discussion.** A "no" just means that your request doesn't fulfill the other person's inner divine qualities. Remembering this opens the door for further exploration and understanding. Find out which inner divine qualities are preventing the other person from saying "yes." Then consider different solutions that might fulfill both of your inner divine qualities.

Going Beyond "No"

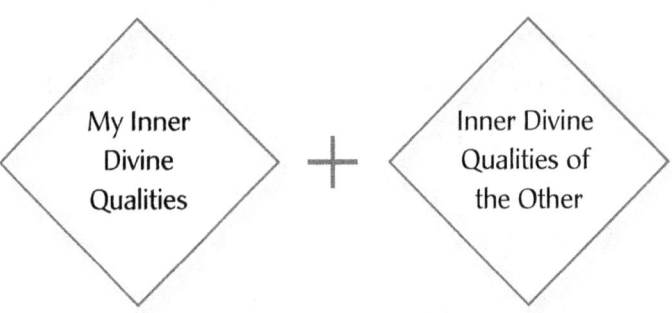

6. **There's always more than one way to fulfill your inner divine qualities.** Remembering this helps us not to make demands or assume that the other person must do what we're asking. We always have other options, even if we don't see them at the moment. Let the solution find you.

MARY MAGDALENE: Respect everyone's free will to choose for themselves what they will do. If they are not choosing to cooperate with you in the way you had in mind, trust in the abundance of the universe, the abundance of God. You will be provided for, perhaps in a way that is so much more wonderful than the way that you were envisioning. Allow God to set your course. You steer the ship, but God sets the course.

Mary Magdalene Beckons,
"The Consciousness of Inclusion," p. 188

Free Will with Children

There's an exception to the principle of respecting the free will of others. If you're responsible for someone who's incapable of making decisions for their highest good, it's your responsibility to make choices for them. The primary arena this applies to is with minor children who haven't yet developed their decision-making abilities. This also applies if you're a caretaker for someone who's mentally incompetent, such as individuals with Alzheimer's or dementia. In both situations a caretaker or guardian needs to make decisions on behalf of others.

This is not to say that it's OK to override another person's free will any time you judge that someone isn't competent to make their own decision. Rather, in these two specific situations—either with minors (children) or with someone who has been medically determined to be incompetent—it's necessary to make decisions and choices on their behalf. With children the situation is temporary. As their ability to engage their free will for the highest good of all develops, they should increasingly be allowed to make their own decisions.

MARY MAGDALENE: Of course, if you are a parent, you are in a position of making decisions for your children, but only to the point that they are not capable. It is very important that you be aware of what they are capable of deciding and respect their choices in these arenas. As they grow, allow them to participate more

> and more in making choices with you, guiding them in learning how to make choices that are for the best for all. And as you see them capable of making their own choices, allow them to do so.
>
> *Mary Magdalene Beckons,* "Responding to Pain," p. 47

When making choices for children, refrain from exerting power as an abstract force over them. Make it clear that you are the one choosing:

Abstract Power: "You *have to* do this."
Owning Your Request: "This is what I've decided" or "This is what I would like you to do. Are you willing to do that?"

Many parents are afraid that their children won't cooperate if they take this approach of speaking from their own choice. They believe it's necessary to assume a position of power-over with children. In my experience, just the opposite is true. Children quickly learn that power is a game. If power-over is used, they soon respond with their own power tactics—whining, complaining, procrastinating, or noncompliance. If we use power with children, we teach them that life is about power, and whoever has the most power wins.

If you want to teach children cooperation and caring for all, don't use power tactics such as demands and threats. Come from your heart. Demonstrate heart-based relating. Explain what you're feeling and the inner divine qualities you're experiencing. Then make requests rather than demands and threats.

If you do this with children, they will respond to your requests. Why? There are a number of reasons. First, your children love you. They actually love pleasing you. You can see this in the way children delight in giving gifts to their parents or asking for validation from their parents/caregivers. Your child's relationship with you is very important to them.

Second, if you share your feelings and inner divine qualities openly with children when you make requests, they will feel your heart. They will then be moved to respond in kind from their heart. This is part of children loving you.

Third, children are aware that they are dependent on you and need your help, but they have to feel safe to show their dependence. When you include their feelings and inner divine qualities in your choices and regularly communicate that inclusion to them, you create a container of safety. You also create safety by making requests rather than demands. Here is an example of relating to children this way:

> "I'm feeling tired and cranky after a hard day of work, and I really need help. I can tell you're hungry and need food. You also seem bored, and I'm guessing you want some fun. How about if I make dinner while you set the table and pick up your toys in the living room, and then after dinner we can play a game together?"

By modeling heart-based relating in your interactions with children, they learn it naturally and will be served by this ability throughout their life.

Practice

JOURNALING

Think of an event that is bringing up feelings for you. Write down:

1. The stimulus (practice being concise)

2. The feelings you're experiencing

3. The inner divine quality that's connected to each feeling

4. One or more requests you could make that would fulfill the inner divine qualities that you listed above

FIVE

Respond from Your Heart

MARY MAGDALENE: To love another is to experience their pain with them, to be fully present for their pain, and to love and open in the midst of that.

This is what I did with Yeshua. I could not remove his pain, nor was it my responsibility to do so. He chose his spiritual path, and mine was to love him and be fully present, heart wide-open to him in his glory and his pain. This is part of the journey of light and love in this dimension.

Mary Magdalene Beckons,
"Releasing Guilt and False Responsibility," p. 232

The next step of the heart path involves responding to the feelings and inner divine qualities of others, or *heart-responding*.

Typical Responses

Most of us never learned how to respond to another from our heart. Instead, we learned other ways to respond, especially when someone is in pain. Here are some of those ways:

1. **Judging.** In situations that have stimulated pain for someone, we often respond with judgment. We look for wrongness and fault, determining what "should" or "shouldn't" have occurred. Responding with judgment keeps us in our mind.

2. **Analyzing.** This involves collecting information about what occurred to determine the cause. This can sound like:

   "How long has this been going on?"
   "When did this begin?"
   "Have you tried this?"
   "The reason this happened is because . . ."

   In collecting information and speculating about causes, we're still staying at the mind level, thus avoiding our feelings and dropping down into them.

3. **Giving Advice.** It is very common to offer advice when someone is in a challenging situation. It can sound like:

   "The best thing to do is . . ."
   "What you should have done is . . ."

   If the advice is unsolicited, it's often unwelcome. Even if the other person is open to your suggestions, giving advice tends to divert the person away from their heart as they focus on actions for "fixing" their problem.

4. **Reassuring.** We may try to comfort the person:

   > "Everything will be fine."
   > "This will all work out."

   Reassuring is like putting a band-aid over the problem. The recipient can sense a hollowness to your assertions since nobody can guarantee a consoling and smooth outcome. More importantly, your reassurance negates their present experience. The other person may go along with your "positive thinking" partly out of hope that you're right and partly to assuage you. But their real pain hasn't been addressed.

5. **Switching the Focus.** Another person's pain may remind us of a similar experience in our own life. This can stimulate us to share our story, to let the person know they're not alone, give encouragement, or suggest possible solutions. This may sound like:

   > "The same thing happened to me . . ."
   > "That reminds me of the time . . ."
   > "I know someone else who that happened to . . ."

   This response, however well meaning, is yet another way of shifting the focus away from the other person and their pain. As a result, they may be left feeling lonely and still disturbed at the heart level.

6. Sympathy. Here we express *our* emotional response to a situation, such as:

"Oh no!"
"That's terrible."
"I'm so sorry."

Sympathy also switches the focus to ourselves. We're expressing *our* emotions, which aren't necessarily the same as the other's. We've again taken the spotlight off the other person, their feelings, and their inner divinity. In fact, they may now feel the need to reassure or take care of *us*, saying things such as, "It's not that bad."

7. Practical Assistance. This is the "let me help" approach, which is another version of trying to fix the problem. Though your genuine desire to be of assistance is often appreciated, it still bypasses the other person's feelings and heart by going straight into action.

All such responses are usually offered with good intentions of giving support. Yet they all bypass the real source of what's occurring, and they circumvent the opportunity to explore and respond from the heart.

The typical responses listed above may be beneficial *after* the person has connected with their heart. But the other person will likely be most helped by *first* connecting with their feelings and inner divinity. Think of this as similar to triage in first aid. What's most necessary is done first.

A Different Way to Respond

When someone expresses pain or distress, they're asking for help. We often assume the help they want is to lessen their pain or to get out of their difficulty. However, Mary says the help they really need is to be more connected to themself and empowered to find their own solution. Heart-responding gives the other person what they truly long for at the heart level.

In connecting with their feelings and inner divine qualities, the person will connect with their own guidance and power. Then they're in the best position to proceed with whatever practical steps *they* choose. After they've completed their process of self-connection and self-determination of the course they want to proceed with, then you may consider sharing your thoughts, feelings, or practical support—if they still seem pertinent and you sense they would be a further contribution.

Heart-Listening

Heart-listening is the first part of heart-responding. In heart-listening we make ourselves 100 percent present for another. For that space of time, we're completely there for them. We consciously set ourself, our ideas, and our concerns aside. We give the other person our undivided attention, fully listening to and hearing what they share. We're not preparing our response. We're not thinking about (or doing) anything else. We're simply present for them, shining the light of our awareness upon them. Presence is a huge gift.

Heart-listening also requires us to engage our "feeling muscle." Part of the practice of heart-listening involves silently guessing the feelings the other person might be having regardless of how they're communicating. They may be "telling the story," judging, analyzing, considering solutions, and so on, but we choose to place our awareness on their underlying feelings. For most of us this is a big shift—from listening with our mind (in the ways suggested earlier) to being centered in the feeling dimension.

Next, we bring our awareness to the source of the person's feelings. We connect each feeling with an inner divine quality that we imagine is causing the feeling. This is what most strongly connects our heart to their heart.

Listening in this way can be very powerful. You'll probably see and understand the other person in a whole new light. And they often feel this connection with you, while also feeling supported in connecting with their own heart. In this sense you're actively "doing" something by silently engaging in this practice.

Heart-Listening

FEELINGS + **INNER DIVINE QUALITIES**

Heart-Reflecting

After heart-listening, you can take the next step of heart-reflecting. In this step you express your guess about the feelings the person is having and the inner divine qualities to which those feelings are connected. You do this in the form of a question to acknowledge the other person's authority about their experiences. The other person is the only one who really knows what they're experiencing. You can make a guess, but they're the authority on themselves. For example, you might ask:

"Are you feeling frustrated because you need cooperation?"

"It sounds like you feel desperate because you want financial security. Is that right?"

"Are you feeling hopeful because you're longing for love?"

I don't recommend asking, "What are you feeling?" because that tends to move people into their head, where they start analyzing their experience. When you provide the feeling and inner divine quality, through your guess, you help them to stay in their heart.

Your guess about the other person's feelings and inner divine qualities doesn't have to be accurate. It only has to be authentic as your best guess. The other will feel the sincerity of your guess. Even if it's wrong, they will use your guess as a springboard to push off from, directing them to the correct feeling and inner divine quality. Thus, your guess will still support the person in identifying their feelings and inner divine qualities. Remember, it's just a guess.

Always begin with guessing the feeling first. If you begin with the inner divine quality, you're likely to come from your mind instead of your heart. After guessing the feeling, link the feeling to an inner divine quality and then check whether your guess is correct. Doing both parts of the process—guessing the feelings *and* inner divine qualities—is the strongest way to make a heart connection.

You'll know when the other person has connected with their heart. They'll often sigh or take a deep breath, followed by a full exhalation. Along with that you'll see a release of physical tension. You can literally see their shoulders relax or their torso drop a little, as though they're letting go down into themselves. The other sign of heart connection is that they'll stop talking about their disturbance or their problem. They won't need to discuss it anymore because they've gotten to the root of their issue and found peace.

At this point the person is often in a deep place. They've connected with something within themselves that's been calling to them, perhaps for a long time. That connection may be tender or fragile. If you sense this, give the person space. It's frequently best to be silent or to affirm that they can take whatever time they need to be in that place. Don't disturb them by talking about your responses, ideas, or suggestions. Hold that until later, after they've completed their process of integrating with this place within themselves, however long that may take.

It's also possible that a person may feel energized and ready to move into action after connecting with their inner divine qualities. Even if the person is initially in the more inward, tender space, eventually, they'll come to this energized state (though that may take hours, days, or weeks). When you sense that someone is energized and ready to act, you can ask whether there are actions they'd like to take to support and maintain this connection with their inner divine quality or qualities. If there are, you can offer suggestions of possible actions, still in the form of a question:

"Would you like to . . .?"
"I'm wondering if it would support you to . . .?"

After all this has been addressed—the person's feelings, inner divine qualities, and possible actions to support their inner divine qualities—they may be available to shift their focus to you, and hear your response to what they've shared. Begin by asking if they'd like to hear what you're thinking or what came up for you. This respects their free will. If they're open to your input, now is the time to share your feelings, ideas, or suggestions.

Skills for Heart-Responding

The first step in developing your skills of heart-responding is to practice listening to your own heart. The more you're able to connect with your feelings and inner divine qualities, the easier it will be to recognize these same feelings and inner divine qualities in others.

When you're ready, expand your practice to include heart-listening to others. Silently guess the feelings and inner divine qualities someone else is having, rather than just going along with their "story" or their thoughts. This form of engagement alone is a big shift from our usual way of listening.

When you feel ready, add the next step to your practice. Offer a heart-response by asking:

> "Are you feeling _____ [name a feeling] because you need _____ [name an inner divine quality]?"

Remember, your guess doesn't have to be correct; it only needs to be sincere.

We tend to guess what would be the case for us in any given situation. But the other person's inner life is unique and not the same as our own. They're often affected by experiences that we haven't had or are not aware of. When guessing another person's feelings and inner divine qualities, do your best to listen deeply to what they're expressing and then reflect that back. It doesn't even need to make sense to you. What matters is that it makes sense to them. Using the same words that the person used can help you stay true to their meaning.

If the other person says your guess isn't accurate, be willing to let go of your idea, and flow with what is the case for them. This is a practice of nonattachment to your own ideas and perspective. I often visualize this as flowing down a stream, being carried by the current rather than swimming to my own destination. Again, your goal is to support the other person's heart connection, not to be "right."

Sometimes the other person will try to make your guess fit, even when it's not accurate. They may hesitate and then offer an ambiguous expression, such as, "Yesssss...," followed by a complex explanation that takes them back into their mind. Signs of tension will be visible in their face as they try to make your guess work. These indications show that your guess wasn't accurate, and the person is simply trying to be accommodating. If you notice these signs—the person becomes more analytical, their energy moves away from their body and up to their head, or there's an increase in bodily tension—hear their answer as a "no" regardless of their words. Gently redirect the conversation back to their feelings, and make a different guess.

Guessing other people's feelings and inner divine qualities can seem daunting at first. To develop proficiency I recommend making use of the lists of feelings and inner divine qualities at the end of this book. You can print them out and even laminate them. Keep them handy. These tools will support you in recognizing your own and others' feelings and inner divine qualities.

Keep in mind that heart-responding is a tool for connection, not a "should." You're in choice in every situation. Perhaps you don't have the energy for engaging this practice in a particular moment, or you may decide heart-responding is not the most supportive option in a given circumstance. The goal is to connect with your heart and the other person's heart, not to burden yourself with something you think you "should" or "have to" do. Explore this practice as you feel moved, and see if it makes your experience with others more fulfilling and productive.

Less Is More

When guessing someone's feelings and inner divine qualities, use as few words as possible. Extra verbiage will tend to send the other person back into their head. To economize on words, keep the stimulus ("When such-and-such happened...") as short as possible. If the stimulus is clear, you can drop it altogether in your response and simply ask about the feelings and inner divine quality:

"Are you feeling _____ [name a feeling] because you want _____ [name an inner divine quality]?"

Then *stop talking*, and give the person as much time as they need to respond.

Sometimes guessing someone's inner divine quality accurately will bring up additional feelings and inner divine qualities for them. In these instances they've gone to a deeper level. This is like an archeological dig where the person goes deeper and deeper, from one inner divine quality to an underlying one. If this happens, stay in the present, letting the person lead you wherever they want to go. Let go of the inner divine quality of the previous moment, and stay with the person as they move on to something new.

At some point the person will come to "a resting place for now." If the situation is very old or a long-standing pattern, this resting place might not be the ultimate bottom level or destination, but it's as far as they can go for today. Coming to that resting place or "shelf" still brings a characteristic sense of peace, signaling that the person is complete for the time being.

Matching Intensity

When guessing someone's feelings, match their intensity. If someone is furious, asking them if they're feeling annoyed can itself feel annoying. If someone is feeling nervous, asking if they're feeling terrified can feel off-putting. When you match the person's intensity of feeling with the feeling word you're using, they feel "gotten" and supported in their self-connection.

Some people are reluctant to acknowledge their feelings. Men often feel uncomfortable revealing their feelings, particularly if they've been shamed in the past for showing feelings. Some people are culturally conditioned not to express feelings. In business settings, it can be viewed as "unprofessional" to express feelings. In such circumstances you can use toned-down feeling words that may feel safer to acknowledge. For example, instead of suggesting that someone feels scared, ask if they feel anxious.

Toned-Down Joyful Feelings

confident	appreciative	refreshed
empowered	moved	rejuvenated
proud	encouraged	rested
secure	optimistic	restored
engaged	inspired	peaceful
absorbed	amazed	calm
alert	wonder	clearheaded
curious		comfortable
fascinated	amused	content
interested	glad	equanimity
intrigued	happy	fulfilled
involved	pleased	mellow
	tickled	quiet
excited		relaxed
eager	friendly	relief
energetic	openhearted	satisfied
enthusiastic	warm	still
exhilarated		
surprised		

Toned-Down Painful Feelings

burnt out	annoyed	vulnerable
exhausted	aggravated	guarded
sleepy	displeased	helpless
tired	frustrated	reserved
weary	impatient	shaky
worn out	irritated	
	irked	confused
disappointed	angry	ambivalent
discouraged	resentful	hesitant
disheartened		perplexed
longing	aversion	puzzled
nostalgic	contempt	torn
	disgusted	
grief	dislike	alienated
hurt	hostile	apathetic
regret	repulsed	bored
		detached
tense	agitated	distant
anxious	disturbed	distracted
irritable	restless	indifferent
nervous	surprised	removed
stressed	troubled	
	uncomfortable	
embarrassed	uneasy	
chagrined	unsettled	
self-conscious	apprehensive	
	suspicious	
	worried	

When Both People Are in Pain

When you're in pain yourself, it's generally not authentic to offer a heart-response to another person. In that circumstance you need your energy and attention for your own self-care. One way to support that self-care is to maintain a space of silence while connecting internally with your own feelings and inner divine qualities. I recommend letting the other person know what you're doing, perhaps through nonverbal cues, such as closing your eyes or raising your index finger, or you can let them know in words.

If you need more time for taking care of yourself, take a break from the other person. Take a walk in nature, write in your journal, meditate, talk to someone else who can offer you support, or do whatever else helps restore you to well-being. Even a few minutes in another space—the hallway or bathroom, your office or bedroom, or simply taking a little distance physically from the other person—may give you the breather you need. Again, I recommend communicating your feelings to the other person and what you'd like to do (i.e., take a break). For example, you can say:

> "I hear that you're upset. I'd like to be present for you and support you, but I don't feel like I can right now because I'm upset too. What I'd like to do is to take thirty minutes apart, so I can give myself some self-care. I'll come back when I'm better able to listen to you and be present for what's going on with you. Would you be willing to do that?"

It's helpful to begin by acknowledging the other person's feelings and inner divine qualities, and affirming that you'd like their needs to be fulfilled. It's also supportive to clarify when you'll return to reengage. You want to return when you're restored through your own self-connection. Then you will have excess for being present for another.

When you recommence, engage heart-listening and heart-responding to the other person. This is similar to Stephen Covey's recommendation: "Seek first to understand, then to be understood." After the other person feels heard and understood, you can share your feelings and inner divine qualities. When you both feel connected to each other's hearts, look for solutions that can fulfill both of your inner divine qualities.

> **MARY MAGDALENE:** Your presence is a blessed gift. Your open heart is the most powerful vessel of transformation, of receiving divine light and empowering it with love. Understand this, but do not stop there. Learn the practices for receiving and transmitting love-light through all these channels, and practice this until it becomes a dance, a joy, a beautiful part of who you are and what you bring to all.
>
> *Mary Magdalene Beckons,*
> "Receiving the Divine Feminine," pp. 18-19

Heart-Responding to Children

Many people ask me if they can use heart-responding with children. My answer is a wholehearted "Yes!" Children understand feelings and inner divine qualities very well as long as you use their language.

> **Adult Language:** "Are you feeling *cautious* because you need *emotional safety*?"
> **Child Language:** "Are you feeling scared because you need to feel safe?"
>
> **Adult Language:** "Are you feeling *frustrated* because you need *autonomy*?"
> **Child Language:** "Are you feeling mad because you want to be able to choose for yourself?"

By talking with children about their feelings and inner divine qualities, you'll be guiding them in connecting with their inner world now and in the future. You'll also be contributing to a future world where people are connected to their heart.

Practice

JOURNALING

1. **Ways of Responding:** Notice your characteristic ways of responding to others. Do you tend to judge (find fault), analyze, give advice, reassure, switch the focus to yourself or others, sympathize, or offer practical help? Write down what you notice.

2. **Practice with a Situation:** Write down a statement that someone has made about you that has stimulated a reaction in you.

Write out different possible responses, as suggested below. Notice how you feel after making each of these responses.

a. Judging or finding fault with the person who made the statement
b. Judging or finding fault with yourself
c. Analyzing or explaining the situation
d. Giving advice
e. Offering reassurance
f. Switching the focus to a related but different "story"
g. Providing sympathy
h. Offering practical help

Now write down:

i. The feelings you're guessing the person was having
j. The inner divine quality you imagine each feeling is emanating from (i.e., the beautiful quality that the other person is either longing for or celebrating)

Notice how you feel after writing out the last two steps.

PRACTICING IN LIFE

Practice being fully present for someone else. Set *yourself* aside as you focus 100 percent on the other person. Silently identify their feelings and the inner divine quality at the root of each feeling. Then silently formulate a heart-response, using this format:

"Are you feeling _____ [name a feeling] because you want _____ [name an inner divine quality]?"

SIX

Include Everyone

> **MARY MAGDALENE:** There is enough for everyone.... And in this consciousness, you discover it is your joy to care for everyone. It is like being part of a family. You care for everyone within the family.
>
> Mary Magdalene Beckons,
"The Consciousness of Inclusion," pp. 185-186

Mary Magdalene is calling us to shift out of a paradigm that humans have been operating from for thousands of years. This old paradigm is based on the assumption of scarcity, the belief, held at a very deep level, that there's not enough for everyone. We believe that if we are to survive, we must compete for limited resources.

The new consciousness that Mary describes is based on abundance and the knowledge that there actually is enough for everyone. She calls this *the consciousness of inclusion*, where everyone's needs and inner divine qualities are tended to. Mary tells us that shifting into the consciousness of inclusion is essential to our spiritual evolution into the fourth dimension and beyond.

The heart wants to include all. In the heart path, we learn that we're only fulfilled when everyone is fulfilled.

Including Everyone

There isn't enough for everyone. We have to compete to survive. ❌

There's enough for everyone. All are included. ♥

Abundance Consciousness

MARY MAGDALENE: There actually is enough for everyone, but to realize this requires a grand shift in consciousness.

Mary Magdalene Beckons,
"The Work for Men—and Many Women, Too," p. 125

Including everyone requires us to be connected with everyone. In the heart path, we do this by first connecting with the feelings and inner divine qualities of each person, before moving into action. This principle is called *connection before action*.

The practice of connection before action is a powerful tool for creating unity and peace. Conflict doesn't exist at the level of our inner divinity. We inherently want this essential aspect of our humanity fulfilled for others. It's like wanting another person to have their arms and legs fully functional, regardless of who that person is or our relationship to them.

Requests such as the following support connection before action:

"Would you reflect back the feelings I'm having and the reasons for those feelings?"

"What comes up for you when you hear this?"

"Say more about that."

As the person responds to these requests, engage heart-listening, silently guessing the feelings the other person is having and the inner divine qualities to which those feelings are connected. When they've finished, heart-reflect back their feelings and inner divine qualities, and ask if what you've understood is accurate.

The possibility of conflict doesn't arise until we shift into action. Conflict simply means that the proposed strategies (actions) don't sufficiently fulfill *everyone's* inner divine qualities. The way out of conflict is to let go of strategizing and go back to connection. Focus again on connecting with everyone's inner divine qualities. Once that heart connection is reestablished, look for *different* solutions that include everyone's inner divine qualities.

Dominators and Submitters

> **MARY MAGDALENE:** You must learn to be as sensitive to others as you are to yourselves, as caring about their needs getting met as you are about your own. It is a major shift into abundance consciousness, as to do this means that you are trusting that there is enough for everyone.
>
> *Mary Magdalene Beckons,*
> "The Work for Men—and Many Women, Too," p. 125

In the 3D paradigm of survival and competition, some people tend to be dominant in expressing and "going after" their inner divine qualities. Others tend to hold back, often because they want ease, comfort, or safety. Think of these two patterns as the *yin* and *yang* of relating.

If we're going to realize the consciousness of inclusion—where everyone's feelings and needs are attended to—we need to change this dynamic of dominance and submission. The first step toward doing this is to become aware of your own tendencies. Do you tend to dominate in relationships or submit?

Below are some suggestions for promoting balance in your interactions with others.

FOR THOSE WHO TEND TO DOMINATE

1. **Find Out How Others Experience You.** Ask others about their experience of you and if you give as much time and space to others as you perceive.

2. **Actively Make Space for Everyone.** Be aware that some people may find it challenging to match your level of communication and participation. Make space for those who are quieter or slower to respond.

   Initially, you may feel like you're holding back, suppressing yourself, or letting others dominate. You may also feel things are taking longer than you enjoy. Eventually, including everyone will feel natural and more fulfilling.

3. **Engage Practices for Including Everyone.** One such practice is to set a fixed amount of time for each person to speak. If someone doesn't use the full time allotted to them, remain in silence for the remainder of their time, holding space for them to speak more if they choose.

   Another supportive practice is to use a "talking piece."[14] An object—such as a special stick or stone or any hand-size object—is designated as the talking piece. Whoever is holding the talking piece has the floor while everyone else remains silent and listens.

   When using a talking piece, give your full attention to whoever is speaking. Send that individual blessing energy to express their greatest truth. Engage in heart-listening, silently connecting with each speaker's feelings and inner divine qualities.

There's also a practice described in the book *Sublime Union*[15] called *the sharing process*.[16] This involves a simple, scripted dialogue to support everyone in being heard. This structured process helps us to receive another person's reality without defense.

MARY MAGDALENE: This does not require that you give up your own desires and needs. What you're giving up is your clinging to these to the exclusion of others. It's the exclusion you are giving up.

Mary Magdalene Beckons,
"The Work for Men—and Many Women, Too," p. 127

FOR THOSE WHO TEND TO SUBMIT

1. **Commit to Participating.** When you don't share what's going on with you, everyone is deprived. We depend on the contributions of each person for our wholeness, as well as for inclusion of everyone. We all bring something different and important. For the well-being of yourself and others, challenge yourself to move beyond your comfort zone and participate.

2. **Stay Connected to Yourself.** Submitters often lose connection to themselves in group situations. It's not until later, when they're alone, that they connect with their feelings and inner divinity. If that's the case for you, practice staying connected to your feelings and inner divine qualities in group situations. Then express what's going on with you, and make active requests for fulfilling your inner divine qualities.

3. **Ask for Help.** Explain to people you interact with regularly that you have a tendency not to participate in social interactions and that you want to change that. Communicate this at a time when your inner divine quality for openness with the other person is being fulfilled. Help the other person understand you by describing what you experience when relating with others. Then make a request for the kind of interaction you'd like, such as:

   > "After you've expressed one idea, I'd like you to pause and check in with me, to see what I have to say about that. I'd like you to listen without interrupting me and wait to respond until I indicate I'm done. Would you be willing to do that?"

4. **Use Nonverbal Cues.** Engage nonverbal cues that indicate you would like to be heard or included. Examples of these include raising your index finger, waving your hand like you're saying "hello," closing your eyes, or touching the other person on the hand or arm. All of these are ways of asking for the other person's attention. Nonverbal communication tends to return people to bodily awareness and, through that, to the present moment with everyone.

5. **Engage Practices that Include Everyone.** The practices described above for doing this (in the "For Those Who Tend to Dominate" section) can also be supportive for those who tend to be submissive:

   a. Agree on a set amount of time for everyone to speak.
   b. Use a talking piece.
   c. Engage the sharing process.

MARY MAGDALENE: This inclusiveness will change your life. It will also change your world. And it is time for this change. Ultimately, it will lead you to God, as God includes all.

Mary Magdalene Beckons,
"The Work for Men—and Many Women, Too," p. 127

More Skills for Inclusion

It may seem counter-intuitive, but in the process of including everyone, it's generally most productive and efficient to focus on one person at a time. This applies to two-person interactions as well as groups of three or more. Connect with one individual's feelings and inner divine qualities fully before focusing on someone else. It's often helpful to reassure whoever isn't currently being heard that everyone will have their time to be listened to.

How do you decide who to begin with? The person in the most pain (having the most emotional charge) needs to be heard first. Those in pain don't have energy and attention for listening to or caring about others. Their focus is on themselves. Once they feel heard about their feelings and inner divine qualities, then their energy and attention is freed up and becomes available for considering the reality of others.

After everyone has been heard, it's helpful to summarize the inner divine qualities of everyone involved. At this stage it's better not to reference the feelings. Returning to the feelings at this point will tend to take people backward to an earlier sense of lack or deprivation that the feelings are describing. Instead, reinforce everyone's connection to what's really important—the beautiful inner divine qualities that people have connected to. This will keep the energy moving forward into the next stage of finding solutions that support everyone's inner divinity.

Just as there's a shift when one person connects with their own inner divinity, there's also a shift in a dyad or group when everyone's inner divine qualities have been identified and included. The sense of connectedness at this juncture is palpable and observable. There can be physical signs of relaxation, body postures that now indicate openness, a softening in people's tone of voice, eye contact between people, and perhaps smiles. All of these are signs that you're now ready to explore actions to support everyone's inner divine qualities.

This experience of unity will often lead to new solutions that hadn't been thought of before. Even if a solution is selected that was previously considered, it will be chosen from a different place—a place of connection to everyone's inner divinity—and that will produce different outcomes.

When seeking solutions, stay open to the emergence of strategies that include everyone. If you have one particular strategy in mind that turns out *not* to fulfill everyone's inner divine qualities, don't get attached to it. Hold your strategies lightly, being willing to modify or let go of them to allow for better solutions to reveal themselves. Ask Spirit to guide you to whatever is for the highest good for all.

Receive Abundantly

> **MARY MAGDALENE:** Your giving to others comes out of your own fullness, your own abundance. Truly, it is God's abundance.... Receive fully of God's abundance, and you will see how that naturally moves you to want to share this abundance with others.
>
> Mary Magdalene Beckons,
> "The Consciousness of Inclusion," p. 186

Many of us believe that wanting something for ourself is "selfish." In holding this belief, we forget that including everyone also means including ourself. Mary Magdalene tells us to fully receive God's abundance. This is the basis for giving to others: we give from our own fullness.

To support our becoming powerful receivers, I recommend the following practice, which I learned from Marshall Rosenburg:

1. **Avoid Deflection.** Often when we're given something, including an appreciation or acknowledgment, our first impulse is to deflect it with a statement, such as, "Oh, it was nothing." Or we might immediately turn the attention back on the other person by thanking them and saying how wonderful they are. These are ways of not receiving, by deflecting the energy away from ourself.

2. **Receive Through Your Breath and Eyes.** Inhale deeply, taking the gift in fully with your breath. As you do this, let your eyes show that you've received a precious gift.

3. **Express Your Feelings and Inner Divine Qualities.** Tell the other person the feelings that have been stimulated in you through receiving their gift and which of your inner divine qualities have been fulfilled. Here are examples of communicating in this way:

"In receiving this scarf from you, I feel *delighted* because it fulfills my love of *beauty* and also gives me a sense of *being cared for.*"

"Hearing your appreciation, I feel *touched* because it validates that what I'm doing is *valuable* and that I'm *contributing to others.*"

Notice how different this way of responding is from just saying "thank you." In expressing the feelings and inner divine qualities that have been fulfilled, we support our own connection to our heart, while also deepening the heart-connection between ourself and the other person.

Apologize from Your Heart

Opening to the abundance of our full humanity, with all our attendant feelings, includes regret. The feeling of regret or remorse points to actions we took that didn't fulfill one (or more) of our inner divine qualities. Acknowledging regret supports healing with ourself and with others. It also supports our growth in becoming the person we want to be.

The common form for acknowledging regret is to say, "I'm sorry." Saying this communicates some degree of contrition, but it doesn't connect us deeply to our heart. Nor does it create a deep heart-connection between ourself and the other person. The following practice for apologizing supports much greater heart-connection and deep healing. This process also comes from Marshall Rosenberg.

1. **Briefly explain what you did that you regret.** Avoid self-judgment about how bad or wrong it was.

2. **Express your present feelings about what you did.** Often the feeling will be regret or remorse, but there may be other feelings, such as embarrassment, pain, or sadness.

3. **Express the inner divine qualities of yours that your feelings are pointing to that weren't fulfilled by the actions you took.**

4. **State what you wish you had done instead.**

5. **Ask the other person what comes up for them when they hear you say this.**

Here's an example of this kind of apology:

"When I think about what I said to you the other night about forgetting my birthday, I feel sad because I want to be kind. I also feel frustrated because I want to be transparent about what's really going on for me, rather than turning what I'm feeling into criticism of you.

"Here's what I wish I had said instead: 'When you told me you forgot my birthday, I felt hurt because I want to matter. I also felt disappointed because I wanted to celebrate and do something special together. Can you tell me what comes up for you when you hear what was really going on for me?'"

Celebrations and Mournings

I want to end with one more process for connecting with everyone, which I also learned from Marshall Rosenberg. This is the practice of *celebrations and mournings*. I treasure this practice because it so directly and efficaciously leads to heart-connection between people.

In the practice of celebrations and mournings, we share our present-time joyful feelings and the inner divine qualities that are fulfilled for us. These are our celebrations. We also share our painful feelings and the inner divine qualities that are not fulfilled. These are our mournings.

In expressing celebrations and mournings, we keep the stimulus (the description of what occurred) as short as possible. This supports us in focusing on our feelings and inner divine qualities.

Here's an example of a mourning:

"When the doctor told me I have cancer, I felt shocked because I value being aware of what's going on with me. I also felt scared because I want well-being. And I felt worried about completing the things that matter to me because it's important to me to fulfill my life's purpose."

Here's an example of a celebration:

"In writing this book, I feel excited because I have hope that it will support people in living from their heart."

The practice of celebrations and mournings can be engaged any time you interact with others. It's also valuable as a structured process in a group, where each person shares their present-time celebrations and mournings. This practice helps focus and connect people at the opening of an event or occasion. It's also a powerful way to close a group meeting, celebrating and mourning the inner divine qualities that were fulfilled or not fulfilled during the meeting.

Practice

JOURNALING

1. **Dominance and Submission:** Consider whether you tend to be dominant or submissive in your interactions with others. Write down what you notice. Ask someone close to you if they agree with you and how they perceive your characteristic tendencies.

2. **Expressing Appreciation:** Think of a situation where someone did something that you appreciated. Write down the feelings that were stimulated and the inner divine qualities that were fulfilled. Then write out how you might express it to that person. Notice how it feels to do this.

3. **Expressing an Apology:** Pick a situation where you have regret about an action you took. Write out a heart-based apology that includes:

   a. A concise description of what you did that you have regret about
   b. Your feelings about what you did
   c. The inner divine qualities that weren't fulfilled through your actions, which your feelings are pointing to
   d. What you wish you had done instead
   e. A request to hear how it is for the other person to receive this from you
   f. How you feel now, after articulating this heart-based apology

PRACTICE BUDDY

Find a practice partner to meet with weekly, and practice the heart-path process together. You can meet in person, by phone, or through a video meeting. Begin with one person sharing what's in their heart. After they share, the other person heart-reflects back what they heard. When the sharing person feels heard and connected with their heart, switch roles. Now the second person shares, followed by a heart-reflection from the listening partner.

Resources

12 Steps of the Heart Path—Principles

1. Living from your heart is a spiritual practice.
2. Living from your heart enriches everyone.
3. Judgments keep us in our head and out of our heart.
4. All feelings are valuable; they guide us to our inner divinity.
5. Joyful feelings tell us our inner divinity is fulfilled; painful feelings tell us we're disconnected from our inner divinity.
6. We can build our "feeling muscle."
7. Inner divine qualities (IDQs) are our bridge to God.
8. Our inner divinity is ultimately fulfilled in God.
9. We all share the same inner divine qualities (IDQs).
10. Everyone is the authority on themselves.
11. Everyone's free will matters.
12. We're truly fulfilled when all are fulfilled.

12 Steps of the Heart Path—Practices

1. Share from your own experience.
2. Express celebrations (things you feel happy about) and mournings (things you feel pain about).
3. Use as few words as possible.
4. Make pure observations, without interpretation of rightness or wrongness.
5. Focus on feelings.
6. Link each feeling to the inner divine quality (IDQ) that's the source of the feeling.
7. Give space for experiencing the inner divine quality (IDQ).
8. Practice "connection before action."
9. Find strategies that support the inner divine qualities (IDQs) of those involved.
10. Engage heart-listening and heart-reflection with others.
11. *Ask* others what they're experiencing or what they want; *ask* if someone is open to hearing your feedback or ideas.
12. Include everyone.

Heart-Expressing

"When I heard/saw [or 'When I think about'] _____ [describe the stimulus],

    I felt/feel _____ [name a feeling]

    because I need/want/value/long for _____ [name an inner divine quality]."

"Would you be willing to _____ [make a request]?"

Heart-Reflecting

"Are you feeling _____ [suggest a feeling]

because you want/need/value/long for _____
[suggest an inner divine quality]?"

Judgment Words

abandoned	insulted	rejected
abused	interrupted	ripped off
attacked	intimidated	shut down
belittled	invalidated	shut out
betrayed	invisible	taken advantage of
blamed	isolated	threatened
bullied	judged	thwarted
cheated	left out	trampled on
coerced	manipulated	tricked
cornered	mistrusted	unappreciated
criticized	misunderstood	unheard
disliked	neglected	unloved
dismissed	overpowered	unseen
distrusted	overworked	unsupported
dumped on	patronized	unwanted
harassed	pressured	used
hassled	provoked	victimized
ignored	put down	violated

appropriate/ inappropriate	good/poor taste	superb/terrible
excellent/poor	mature/immature	terrific/dreadful
great/awful	respectful/ disrespectful	valuable/worthless
humane/inhumane	responsible/ irresponsible	wonderful/horrible
		worthy/unworthy

good/bad	should/shouldn't	deserve
right/wrong	must/must not	never/always
	have to	

Joyful Feelings

AFFECTIONATE
compassionate
friendly
loving
open-hearted
sympathetic
tender
warm

ENGAGED
absorbed
alert
curious
engrossed
enchanted
entranced
fascinated
interested
intrigued
involved
spellbound
stimulated

HOPEFUL
expectant
encouraged
optimistic

JOYFUL
amused
delighted
glad
happy
jubilant
pleased
tickled

EXCITED
amazed
animated
ardent
aroused
astonished
dazzled
eager
energetic
enthusiastic
giddy
invigorated
lively
passionate
surprised
vibrant

GRATEFUL
appreciative
moved
thankful
touched

INSPIRED
amazed
awed
wonder

CONFIDENT
empowered
open
proud
safe
secure

EXHILARATED
blissful
ecstatic
elated
enthralled
exuberant
radiant
rapturous
thrilled

PEACEFUL
calm
clearheaded
comfortable
centered
content
equanimous
fulfilled
mellow
quiet
relaxed
relieved
satisfied
serene
still
tranquil
trusting

REFRESHED
enlivened
rejuvenated
renewed
rested
restored
revived

This chart is based upon the Feelings Inventory from the Center for Nonviolent Communication.
© 2005 by Center for Nonviolent Communication, www.cnvc.org.

Painful Feelings

FATIGUE
beat
burnt out
depleted
exhausted
lethargic
listless
sleepy
tired
weary
worn out

ANNOYED
Aggravated
dismayed
disgruntled
displeased
exasperated
frustrated
impatient
irritated
irked

ANGRY
enraged
furious
incensed
indignant
irate
livid
outraged
resentful

AVERSION
animosity
appalled
contempt
disgusted
dislike
hate
horrified
hostile
repulsed

CONFUSED
ambivalent
baffled
bewildered
dazed
hesitant
lost
mystified
perplexed
puzzled
torn

VULNERABLE
fragile
guarded
helpless
insecure
leery
reserved
sensitive
shaky

DISCONNECTED
alienated
aloof
apathetic
bored
cold
detached
distant
distracted
indifferent
numb
removed
uninterested
withdrawn

EMBARRASSED
ashamed
chagrined
flustered
guilty
mortified
self-conscious

YEARNING
envious
jealous
longing
nostalgic
pining
wistful

Painful Feelings *(continued)*

AFRAID	SAD	DISQUIET
apprehensive	depressed	agitated
dread	dejected	alarmed
foreboding	despair	discombobulated
frightened	despondent	disconcerted
mistrustful	disappointed	disturbed
panicked	discouraged	perturbed
petrified	disheartened	rattled
scared	forlorn	restless
suspicious	gloomy	shocked
terrified	heavy hearted	startled
wary	hopeless	surprised
worried	melancholy	troubled
	unhappy	turbulent
TENSE	wretched	turmoil
anxious		uncomfortable
cranky	**PAIN**	uneasy
distressed	agony	unnerved
distraught	anguished	unsettled
edgy	bereaved	upset
fidgety	devastated	
frazzled	grief	
irritable	heartbroken	
jittery	hurt	
nervous	lonely	
overwhelmed	miserable	
restless	regretful	
stressed out	remorseful	

This chart is based upon the Feelings Inventory from the Center for Nonviolent Communication.
© 2005 by Center for Nonviolent Communication, www.cnvc.org.

Toned-Down Joyful Feelings

confident
empowered
proud
secure

engaged
absorbed
alert
curious
fascinated
interested
intrigued
involved

excited
eager
energetic
enthusiastic
exhilarated
surprised

appreciative
moved
encouraged
optimistic

inspired
amazed
wonder

amused
glad
happy
pleased
tickled

friendly
openhearted
warm

refreshed
rejuvenated
rested
restored

peaceful
calm
clearheaded
comfortable
content
equanimity
fulfilled
mellow
quiet
relaxed
relief
satisfied
still

Toned-Down Painful Feelings

burnt out
exhausted
sleepy
tired
weary
worn out

disappointed
discouraged
disheartened
longing
nostalgic

grief
hurt
regret

tense
anxious
irritable
nervous
stressed

embarrassed
chagrined
self-conscious

annoyed
aggravated
displeased
frustrated
impatient
irritated
irked
angry
resentful

aversion
contempt
disgusted
dislike
hostile
repulsed

agitated
disturbed
restless
surprised
troubled
uncomfortable
uneasy
unsettled
apprehensive
suspicious
worried

vulnerable
guarded
helpless
reserved
shaky

confused
ambivalent
hesitant
perplexed
puzzled
torn

alienated
apathetic
bored
detached
distant
distracted
indifferent
removed

Inner Divine Qualities

CONNECTION
acceptance
affection
appreciation
belonging
cooperation
communication
closeness
community
companionship
compassion
consideration
consistency
empathy
inclusion
intimacy
love
mutuality
nurturing
respect
safety
security
stability
support
to know and
 be known
to see and be seen
to understand and
 be understood
trust
warmth

PHYSICAL WELL-BEING
air
food
movement/exercise
rest/sleep
sexual expression
safety
shelter
touch
water

HONESTY
authenticity
integrity
presence

PLAY
joy
humor

PEACE
beauty
communion
ease
equality
harmony
inspiration
order

MEANING
awareness
celebration of life
challenge
clarity
competence
consciousness
contribution
creativity
discovery
efficacy
effectiveness
growth
hope
learning
mourning
participation
purpose
self-expression
stimulation
to matter
understanding

AUTONOMY
choice
freedom
independence
space
spontaneity

This chart is drawn from the Needs Inventory by the Center for Nonviolent Communication.
© 2005 by Center for Nonviolent Communication, www.cnvc.org.

Notes

1. Mary Magdalene was a follower of Jesus in the Bible. Many believe she was Jesus's wife.

2. "Yeshua" is the Hebrew/Aramaic name for Jesus. Many believe Jesus was called Yeshua 2,000 years ago, in Israel. In Mercedes' channeled sessions, Mary Magdalene has always called Jesus "Yeshua." Accordingly, the name Yeshua is used in this book.

3. For more information about the book, *Mary Magdalene Beckons*, go to www.mercedeskirkel.com.

4. For more information about Nonviolent Communication (NVC), go to www.cnvc.org.

5. Later in his work, Marshall Rosenberg revealed a spiritual basis for NVC, as he saw it; this is described in the book *Practical Spirituality* (PuddleDancer Press, 2005).

6. For a full discussion of the twelve dimensions of our universe, see *Mary Magdalene Beckons* by Mercedes Kirkel.

7. The Heart Path video course follows the chapters in this book, with one video for each chapter. For more information about the video course, go to www.mercedeskirkel.com.

8. *Mary Magdalene Beckons* can be found at www.mercedeskirkel.com.

9. The Feminine and the Masculine are key concepts in the teaching of Yeshua and Mary Magdalene. The terms refer to the archetypal Feminine and Masculine that reside within all of us (regardless of our gender) and within all of manifestation. The twin concepts are similar to the

concepts of yin and yang in Eastern philosophy. Yeshua and Mary use the terms "Divine Feminine" or "Divine Masculine" when referring to the Feminine or Masculine aspects of God or our human divinity.

The Feminine aspects of our humanness relate to our body, energy, emotions, sexuality, and heart. The highest form of the Feminine is pure love. The Masculine aspects of our humanity relate to the mind and willpower. The highest form of the Masculine is pure consciousness.

Yeshua and Mary Magdalene teach that to transition into the fourth dimension, a being must become strong in all aspects of both the Feminine and the Masculine, which includes coming into balance, harmony, and union between the Feminine and the Masculine. An in-depth explanation of the Masculine and the Feminine can be found in *Mary Magdalene Beckons* by Mercedes Kirkel.

10. *Mary Magdalene Beckons* can be found at www.mercedeskirkel.com.

11. This process for connecting with the fullness of our inner divine qualities was developed by the NVC teacher Robert Gonzales.

12. This is a quote from Marshall Rosenberg, the founder of Nonviolent Communication (NVC), from whom I first learned about not requiring others to mind read.

13. This precept also came from Marshall Rosenberg: There is always more than one way to fulfill our inner divine qualities.

14. The use of a talking piece originated with Native Americans as a sacred practice for listening and connecting when they were in circle together.

15. The book *Sublime Union* can be found at www.mercedeskirkel.com.

16. The "sharing process" is explained on pages 52-55 of *Sublime Union* by Mercedes Kirkel. For more information about *Sublime Union*, go to www.mercedeskirkel.com.

About the Author

MERCEDES KIRKEL is a multi-award-winning, bestselling author and channel for Mary Magdalene and Yeshua.

In the summer of 2010, Mary Magdalene began coming to Mercedes daily, giving extraordinary messages for humanity's evolution and spiritual growth. That was the birth of the first book in the Magdalene-Yeshua Teachings, *Mary Magdalene Beckons: Join the River of Love*. Since then, Mary Magdalene and Yeshua have continued to communicate through Mercedes, delivering illuminating messages about the sacred partnership of the Divine Feminine and Masculine and guiding people in their spiritual development.

Based in New Mexico, Mercedes offers online courses, events, and private sessions. Her specialties include heart coaching and spiritual support.

Learn more about Mercedes and her work at:
www.mercedeskirkel.com.

Books and Videos by Mercedes Kirkel

THE HEART PATH VIDEO COURSE

A video course of Mercedes coaching people in the heart path, using exercises and real-life demonstrations

THE MAGDALENE-YESHUA TEACHING BOOKS

Mary Magdalene Beckons:
Join the River of Love (Book One)

Sublime Union:
A Woman's Sexual Odyssey Guided by Mary Magdalene (Book Two)

Dialogues with Yeshua and Mary Magdalene:
The Journey to Love (Book Three)

The Heart Path of Mary Magdalene:
A Guide to Living from Your Heart (Book Four)

Forthcoming:
The Holy Grail of Yeshua and Mary Magdalene:
The Quest of Love (Book Five)

All available at: www.mercedeskirkel.com

www.ingramcontent.com/pod-product-compliance
Lightning Source LLC
Chambersburg PA
CBHW072049290426
44110CB00014B/1604